Create a Bright and Inviting Home!

Flower Basket Pillow

Instructions on page 33.

Old Rose Tablecloth
Instructions on page 36.

Red Rose Tablecloth
Instructions on page 38.

Blue Rose Table Center
Instructions on page 40.

Table Runner
Instructions on page 44.

Crocus Runner

Instructions on page 45.

Wild Flower Pillow
Instructions on page 64.

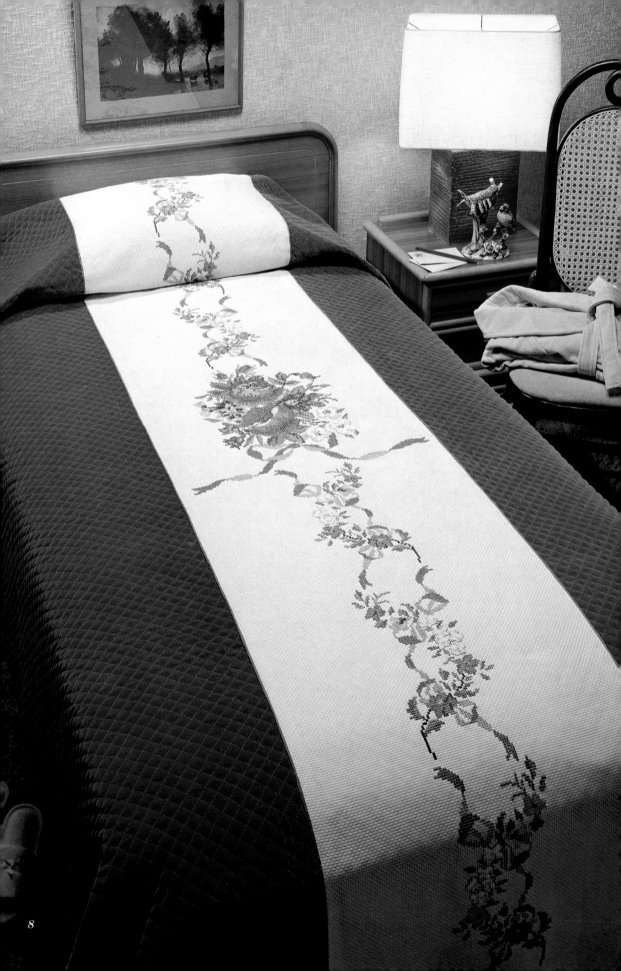

Pillows
Instructions on page 48.

Bedspread
Instructions on page 58.

Table Runner and Placemats

Instructions on page 85.

Flower Garden Table Center

Instructions on page 52.

Narcissus Table Center
Instructions on page 62.

13

Coasters

Instructions on page 66.

Grape Table Center and Matching Mat

Instructions on page 42.

Tulip Pillows

Instructions on page 47.

Bedspread

Instructions on page 73.

Lovely Designs

Castle Panel
Instructions on page 71.

Piano Cover

Instructions on page 68.

Small Flower Table Runner

Instructions on page 54.

Violet Table Runner

Instructions on page 76.

Napkins, Doily, and Coasters
Instructions on page 92.

Oval Doily
Ⓐ Instructions on page 72.

Octagon Doily
Ⓑ Instructions on page 67.

Square Doily
Ⓒ Instructions on page 84.

UNFORGETTABLE GIFTS TO MAKE

Christmas Wall Hanging
Instructions on page 80.

Fruit Wall Hanging
Instructions on page 81.

Rabbit Panel

Instructions on page 102.

Doll House Panel

Instructions on page 90.

Lampshade Panel
Instructions on page 57.

Street Panel
Instructions on page 56.

Bridge Panel
Instructions on page 96.

Flower Garden Album

A Instructions on page 99.

A

Cattleya Album
B Instructions on page 78.

Petite Fleur Album
C Instructions on page 98.

B

C

Slippers
Instructions on page 103.

32

Instructions

Flower Basket Pillow, *shown on page 1.*

MATERIALS: Beige Aida cloth (35 vertical and horizontal threads per 10cm square), 91cm by 48.5cm. D.M.C. 6-strand embroidery floss, No. 25: See Color Key for colors and amounts. Inner pillow, 45cm square, stuffed with 500g kapok. 40cm-long zipper.

FINISHED SIZE: 44.5cm by 44.5cm square.

DIRECTIONS: Find center point of FRONT piece and begin working cross-stitches from center. Follow chart for placement of colors. Sew together marked ends of BACK pieces. Sew on zipper. With right sides facing, fold as shown and stitch along stitching lines. Turn to right side. Insert inner pillow.

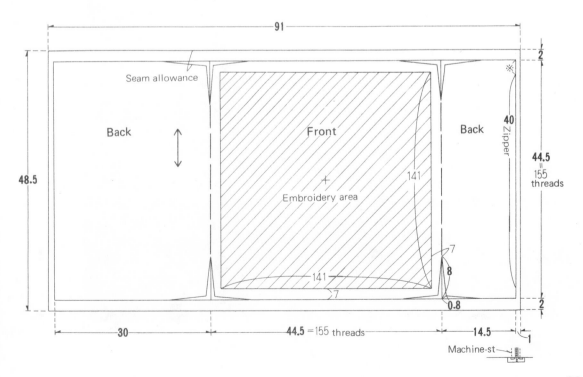

COLOR KEY

Use 5 strands of floss unless otherwise indicated.

Color No. Skeins

Tints of Green

▲ = 319   1
ℓ = 320   1
• = 368   1
V = 471   1
● = 580   1
△ = 3345   1

Beaver gray

O = 648   4

Cream

X = 746   4

Tints of Brown

◉ = 830   1
☰ = 831   1
▯ = 831 (Holbein St.)
◆ = 839   1
⊘ = 839 (Use 1 strand.)
◎ = 841   1
⊠ = 841 (1 strand.)
◕ = 938 Small amount

Tints of Pink

Y = 304   Small amount
Z = 309   1
II = 776   1
◢ = 814   1
◑ = 816   0.5
— = 818   1
L = 961   1
< = 3326   0.5
U = 3354   1
⬗ = 3687   1

Tints of Yellow

⊞ = 307   1
+ = 725   1
⦶ = 727   1
I = 782   1

Tints of Red

⊠ = 3041   0.5
C = 3042   0.5

Tints of Blue

T = 334   1
■ = 796   1
✕ = 798   1
S = 800   1

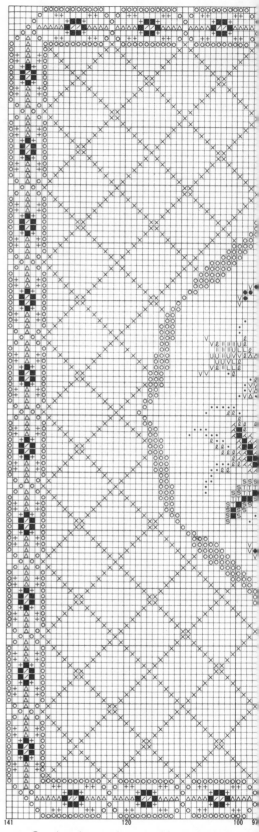

141   120   100 97

One-thread square is counted for each stitch.

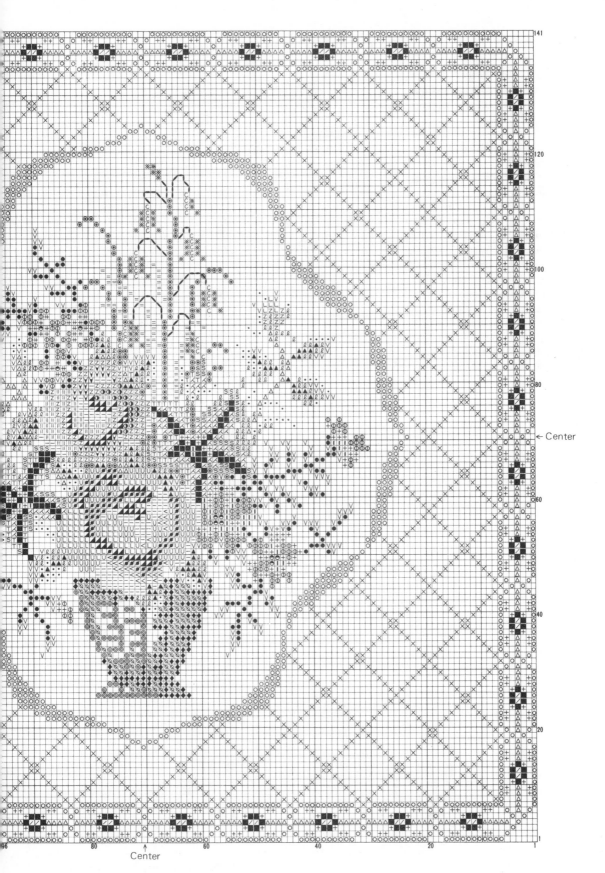

← Center

Center

Old Rose Tablecloth, *shown on page 2.*

MATERIALS: Beige Aida cloth (35 vertical and horizontal threads per 10cm square), 91.4cm by 244cm. D.M.C. 6-strand embroidery floss, No. 25: See Color Key for colors and amounts.

FINISHED SIZE: 114.5cm by 114.5cm square.

DIRECTIONS: 1. Cut fabric as shown on next page. 2. Sew two peices together along the selvages. Press seam open. 3. Find center point of fabric and select embroidery area. Work scroll patterns first. Work in cross-stitch, following chart for placement of colors. 4. To finish, turn back 0.7cm and 2.9cm hem on all edges, miter corners and slip-stitch (see page 109).

COLOR KEY

Use 6 strands of floss.

Color No. Skeins

Tints of Red

O	= 223	5
S	= 224	5
◩	= 225	3
●	= 315	3
◡	= 315 (Use 3 strands & Holbein St.)	

Tints of Green

II	= 472	2
◢◣	= 3011	3
◸	= 3012	6
−	= 3013	3
◆	= 3051	1

Beige

⊠	= 3046	6
◼		

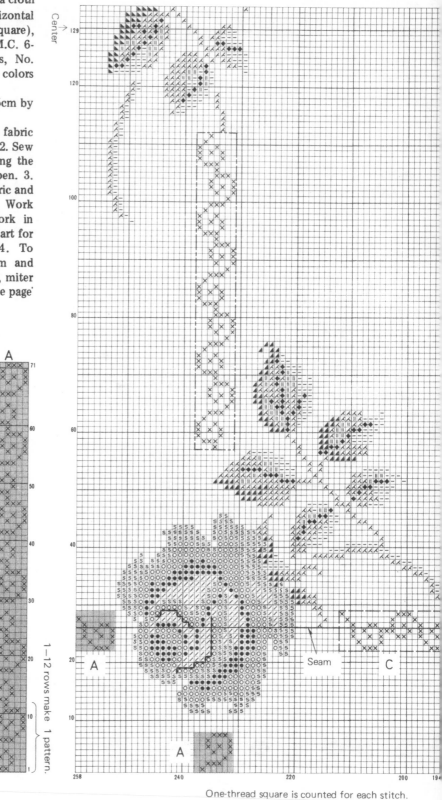

One-thread square is counted for each stitch.

36

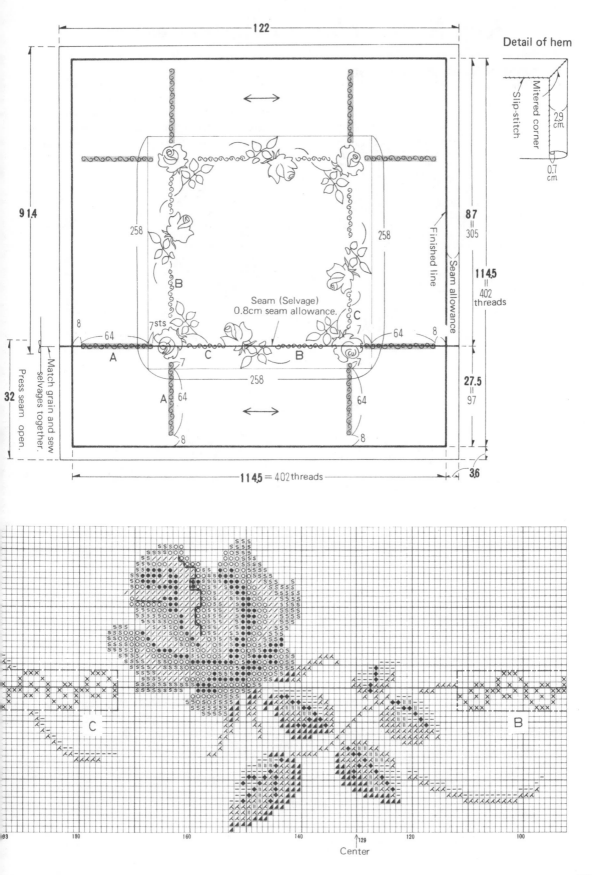

122

Detail of hem

Mitered corner

Slip-stitch

29 cm

0.7 cm

91.4

258

258

87 = 305

Finished line

Seam allowance

114.5 = 402 threads

B

Seam (Selvage)
0.8cm seam allowance.

C

8

64

7sts

A

C

B

7

C

258

A

64

7

64

27.5 = 97

8

8

Match grain and sew
selvages together.

Press seam open.

32

114.5 = 402 threads

3.6

C

B

193   180   160   140   129   120   100

Center

37

Red Rose Tablecloth, *shown on page 3.*

MATERIALS: Beige Indian cloth (52 vertical and horizontal threads per 10cm square), 91cm by 91cm square. D.M.C. 6-strand embroidery floss, No. 25: See Color Key for colors and amounts.

FINISHED SIZE: 84cm by 84cm square.

DIRECTIONS: Find center point of fabric and select embroidery area. Work in cross-stitch, following chart. To finish, turn back 1cm and 2.5cm hem on all edges, miter corners and slip-stitch (see page 109).

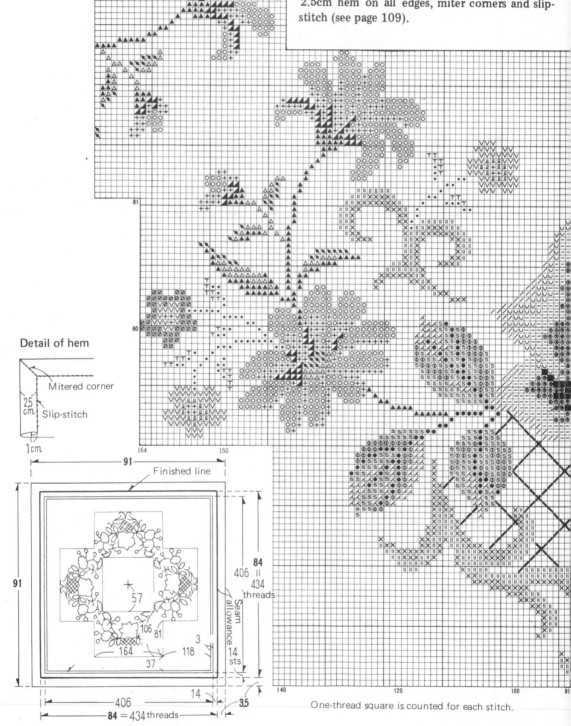

Detail of hem

Mitered corner

2.5 cm

Slip-stitch

1cm

One-thread square is counted for each stitch.

COLOR KEY

Use 4 strands of floss.

Color No. Skeins

Tints of Brown		Tints of Green		Tints of Yellow		Tints of Red	
⊞ II = 613	3	S = 367	2	O = 744	5	− = 3328	3
☒ = 611	4	Φ = 368	2	+ = 725	2	◉ = 347	2
◢ = 611 (Holbein St.)		● = 319	1.5	◢ = 783	1	⧄ = 754	1
		• = 500	1			U = 760	2
		T = 501	1	**Tints of Blue**		■ = 902	0.5
		⋌ = 502	1	ℓ = 930	1		
		▲ = 936	2	V = 931	2	**Corn yellow**	
		◣ = 3013	1	Ø = 932	1	I = 712	1
		△ = 3052	1				

81
60
40
1
90
80
60
40
20
1
Center
Design for border
Center

Blue Rose Table Center, *shown on page 4.*

MATERIALS: Beige Indian cloth (52 vertical and horizontal threads per 10cm square), 67cm by 67cm square. D.M.C. 6-strand embroidery floss, No. 25: See Color Key for colors and amounts. Beige braid, 1.5cm by 280cm.

FINISHED SIZE: 66cm by 66cm square (including braid).
DIRECTIONS: 1. Cut fabric as indicated. 2. Find center point of fabric and select embroidery area. Work in cross-stitch, following chart. 3. Sew on braid as indicated.

COLOR KEY

Use 4 strands of floss.
Color No. Skeins

Tints of Blue				Tints of Purple		Tints of Blue-gray	
◉=312 2	─=747 0.5	T=799 1	O=826 1.5	ℓ=208 1	X=336 2
▱=312 (Holbein St.)	X=792 1.5	⁄=800 1	‖=827 1	U=209 1	◢=930 2
◤=334 1.5	V=794 1	S=813 1	+=996 0.5	⋌=210 1.5	Φ=931 2
L=322 1.5	◎=797 0.5	■=820 0.5	I=3325 2	•=211 1	<=932 2
Z=519 0.5	△=798 1.5	▲=824 1		●=327 1	+ = White-Small amou...

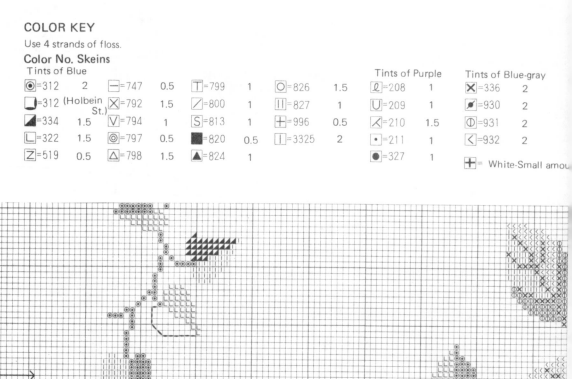

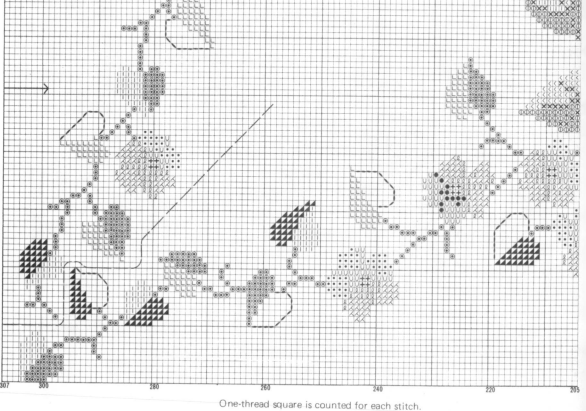

One-thread square is counted for each stitch.

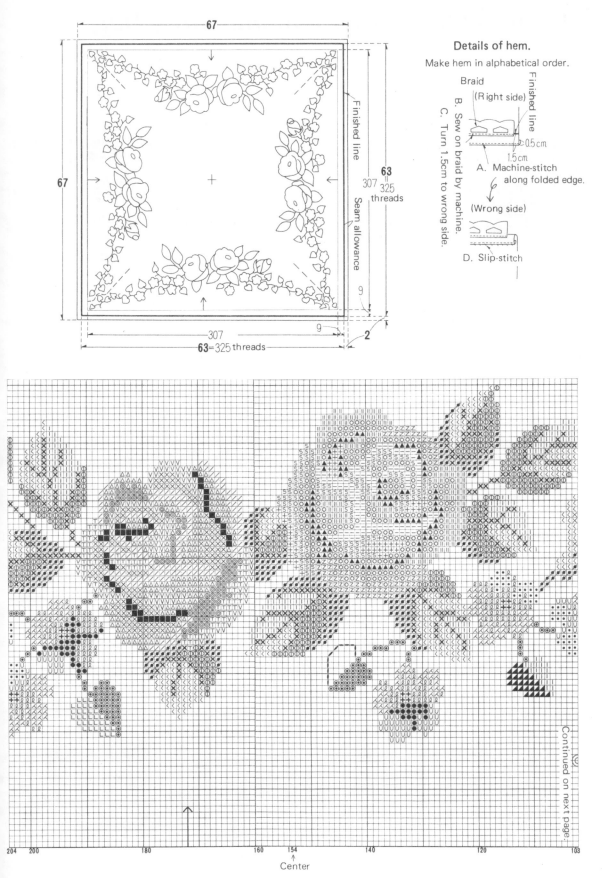

67

67

63

307 ÷ 325 threads

307

63 = 325 threads

9

9

2

Finished line

Seam allowance

Finished line

Details of hem.

Make hem in alphabetical order.

Braid

(Right side)

Finished line

0.5 cm

1.5 cm

B. Sew on braid by machine.

C. Turn 1.5cm to wrong side.

A. Machine-stitch
along folded edge.

(Wrong side)

D. Slip-stitch

Continued on next page.

204 200   180   160 154   140   120   103

Center

Grape Table Center and Matching Mat,

shown on page 15.

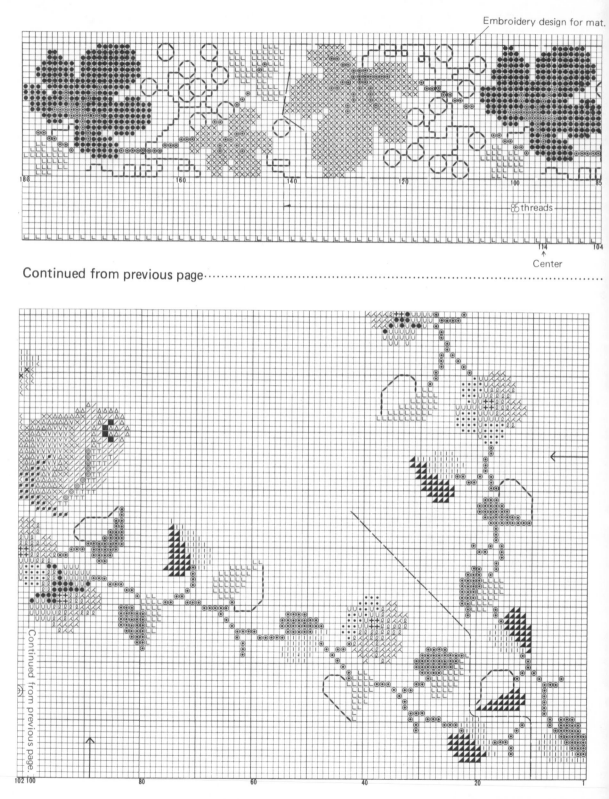

Embroidery design for mat.

188   160   140   120   100   85

85 threads

114
↑
Center

Continued from previous page

Continued from previous page.

102 100   80   60   40   20   1

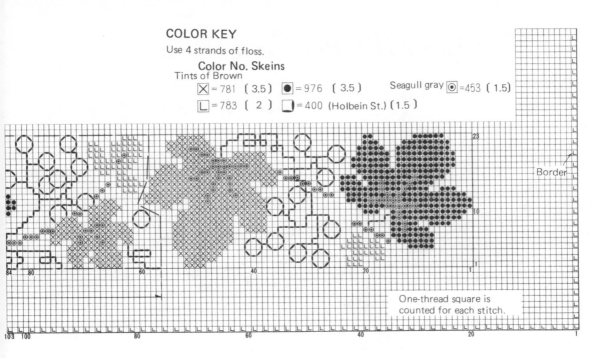

COLOR KEY

Use 4 strands of floss.

Color No. Skeins

Tints of Brown

☒ = 781 (3.5) ● = 976 (3.5) Seagull gray ◎ = 453 (1.5)

☐ = 783 (2) ☐ = 400 (Holbein St.) (1.5)

Border

23

10

1

84 80 60 40 20

One-thread square is counted for each stitch.

103 100 80 60 40 20 1

MATERIALS: Beige Aida cloth (35 vertical and horizontal threads per 10cm square), 83 cm by 48cm for Table Center and 42.5cm by 26cm for Mat. D.M.C. 6-strand embroidery floss, No. 25: See Color Key for colors and amounts.

FINISHED SIZE: Table Center, 41cm by 72cm. Mat, 22cm by 36.5cm.

DIRECTIONS: For Table Center: Choose embroidery area by counting the threads of fabric. Work the cross-stitch design, following chart. To finish, turn back hem on all edges and slip-stitch. For Mat: Find center point of fabric and work cross-stitches, following chart. Make hem in same manner as for Table Center.

Table Center

83

Seam allowance

48

Finished line Border

11 19

61

188

23

20 ★ 85 11 19

129 41 = 143 threads

7

3.5

227

12

72 = 251 threads

5.5

Mat

42.5

26 Seam allowance Finished line Border

13 20

23

★ 85 15

22

22 = 65 = 77 threads

6

2

113

7

36.5 = 127 threads

3

43

Table Runner, *shown on page 5.*

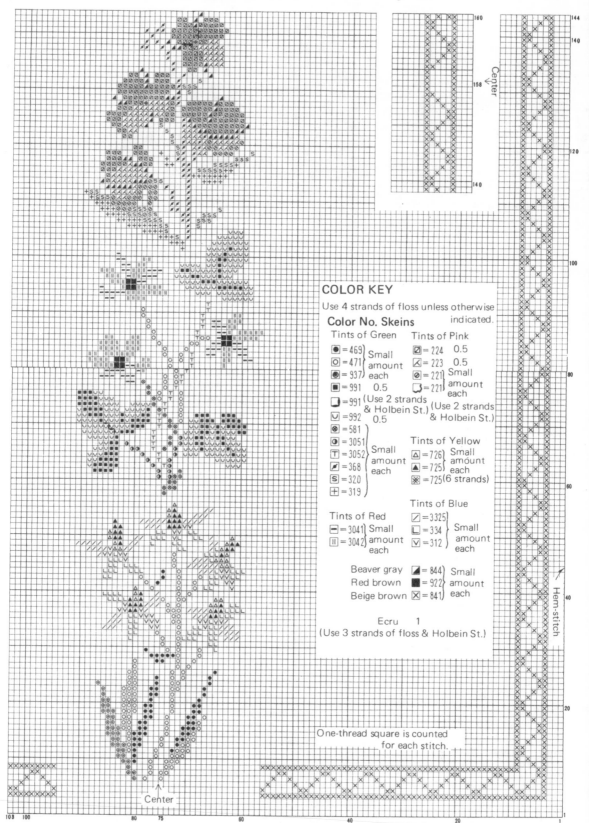

COLOR KEY

Use 4 strands of floss unless otherwise indicated.

Color No. Skeins

Tints of Green
- ◑ = 469 ⎫ Small
- ◎ = 471 ⎬ amount
- ◉ = 937 ⎭ each
- ■ = 991
- ▢ = 991 0.5 (Use 2 strands & Holbein St.)
- ⋃ = 992 0.5
- ⊛ = 581
- ◨ = 3051 ⎫
- T = 3052 ⎬ Small amount each
- ⊿ = 368 ⎪
- S = 320 ⎪
- ✛ = 319 ⎭

Tints of Pink
- ⊿ = 224 0.5
- ⊠ = 223 0.5
- ⊘ = 221 ⎫ Small amount each
- ⏝ = 221 ⎭ (Use 2 strands & Holbein St.)

Tints of Yellow
- △ = 726 ⎫ Small amount each
- ▲ = 725 ⎬
- ✳ = 725 (6 strands)

Tints of Blue
- ⊘ = 3325 ⎫
- L = 334 ⎬ Small amount each
- V = 312 ⎭

Tints of Red
- ⊟ = 3041 ⎫ Small amount each
- ‖ = 3042 ⎭

- Beaver gray ◪ = 844 ⎫ Small
- Red brown ■ = 922 ⎬ amount
- Beige brown ⊠ = 841 ⎭ each

Ecru   1
(Use 3 strands of floss & Holbein St.)

One-thread square is counted for each stitch.

Center

Center

Hem-stitch

44

MATERIALS: Natural-colored Aida cloth (41 vertical and horizontal threads per 10cm square), 91cm by 51cm. D.M.C. 6-strand embroidery floss, No. 25: See Color Key for colors and amounts.
FINISHED SIZE: 83cm by 43cm.
DIRECTIONS: Find center point of fabric and work in cross-stitch, following chart. To finish, turn back 1cm and 3cm hem on all edges, miter corners and hem-stitch (see page 109).

Crocus Runner,
shown on page 6.

MATERIALS: Navy Aida cloth (41 vertical and horizontal threads per 10cm square), 91cm by 33cm. D.M.C. 6-strand embroidery floss, No. 25: See Color Key for colors and amounts.
FINISHED SIZE: 86cm by 28cm.
DIRECTIONS: Decide embroidery area by counting threads of fabric. Work in cross-stitch, following chart. To finish, turn back 1cm and 1.5cm hem on all edges, miter corners and slip-stitch (see page 109).

Detail of hem

1 cm — 3cm
Hem-stitch — Mitered corner

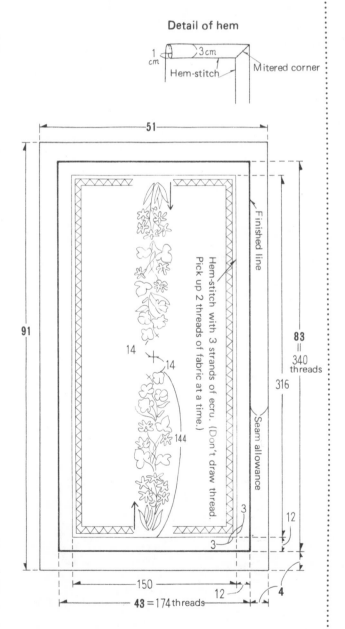

Detail of hem

1 cm — 1.5cm
Slip-stitch — Mitered corner

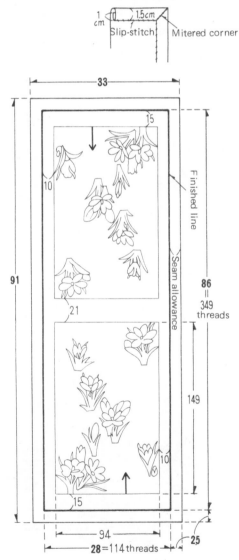

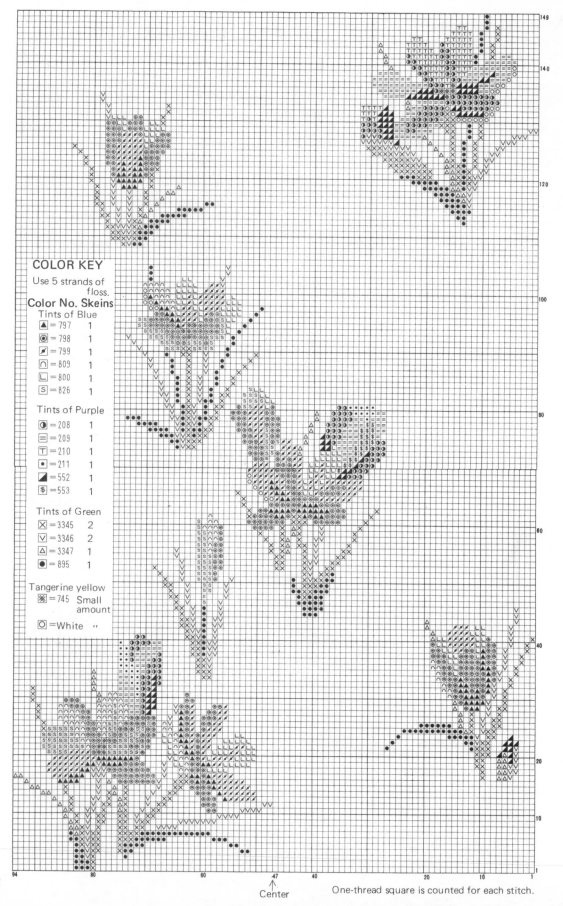

COLOR KEY

Use 5 strands of floss.

Color No. Skeins

Tints of Blue

▲ = 797   1
◉ = 798   1
⬛ = 799   1
∩ = 809   1
L = 800   1
S = 826   1

Tints of Purple

◐ = 208   1
= = 209   1
T = 210   1
• = 211   1
◣ = 552   1
$ = 553   1

Tints of Green

⊠ = 3345   2
∨ = 3346   2
△ = 3347   1
● = 895   1

Tangerine yellow

※ = 745   Small amount

⊙ = White   "

Center

One-thread square is counted for each stitch.

Tulip Pillows, *shown on page 16.*

MATERIALS FOR ONE PILLOW: Navy Aida cloth (41 vertical and horizontal threads per 10cm square), 90cm by 47cm. D.M.C. 6-strand embroidery floss, No. 25: See Color Key for colors and amounts. Inner pillow, 45cm square, stuffed with 450g kapok. 39cm-long zipper.

FINISHED SIZE: 43cm by 43cm square.

DIRECTIONS: 1. Find the center point of FRONT piece and work in cross-stitch, following chart. 2. Sew ends of BACK pieces together and sew on zipper. 3. With right sides facing, stitch along stitching lines. Turn to right side. Insert inner pillow.

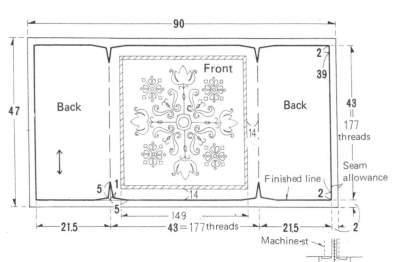

COLOR KEY

Use 4 strands of floss.

	R	L	Skeins
✎	351	742	1
△	353	744	0.5
T	644	644	0.5
◉	741	817	0.5
●	797	797	0.5
⊠	799	799	0.5
▲	817	740	1
⁄	819	White	0.5
○	911	704	1
✕	931	931	1.5

Center

One-thread square is counted for each stitch.

Pillows, *shown on page 9.*

MATERIALS FOR ONE PILLOW: Beige Aida cloth (41 vertical and horizontal threads per 10cm square), 91cm by 48cm. D.M.C. 6-strand embroidery floss, No. 25: See Color Key for colors and amounts. Inner pillow 45cm square, stuffed with 500g kapok. 36cm-long zipper. Cotton cord, 1cm by 200cm (pink for Strawberry pillow and dark red for Grape pillow).

FINISHED SIZE: 43cm by 43cm square.

DIRECTIONS: 1. Find center point of FRONT piece and work in cross-stitch, following chart. 2. Sew ends of BACK pieces (3.5cm) together and sew on zipper. 3. With right sides facing, stitch along stitching lines. Turn to right side. Sew on cotton cord. 4. Insert inner pillow.

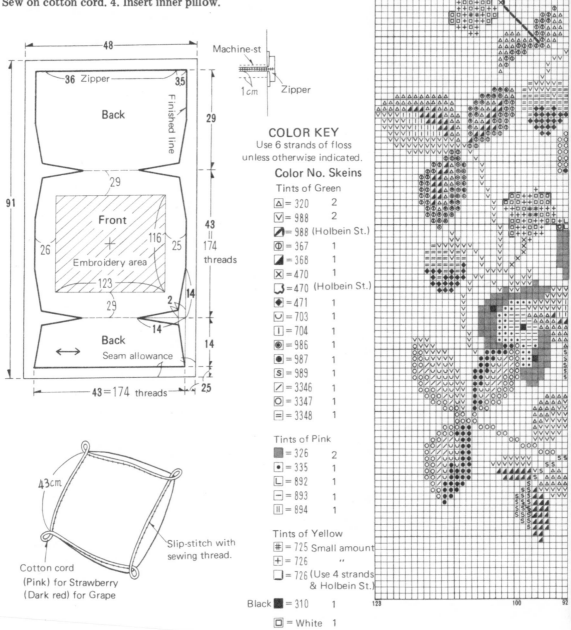

COLOR KEY
Use 6 strands of floss
unless otherwise indicated.

	Color No.	Skeins
Tints of Green		
△ =	320	2
∨ =	988	2
∕ =	988	(Holbein St.)
◍ =	367	1
◢ =	368	1
✕ =	470	1
⌇ =	470	(Holbein St.)
◆ =	471	1
∪ =	703	1
∏ =	704	1
◉ =	986	1
● =	987	1
S =	989	1
∕ =	3346	1
O =	3347	1
= =	3348	1
Tints of Pink		
▨ =	326	2
• =	335	1
L =	892	1
− =	893	1
∥ =	894	1
Tints of Yellow		
⊞ =	725	Small amount
+ =	726	"
☐ =	726	(Use 4 strands & Holbein St.)
Black ▆ =	310	1
☐ =	White	1

One-thread square is counted for each stitch.

← Center

Center

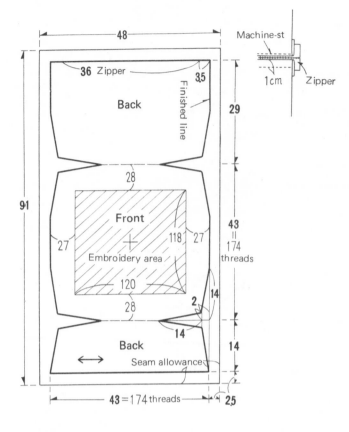

Machine-st

1cm   Zipper

COLOR KEY

Use 6 strands of floss.

Color No. Skeins

Tints of Green			Tints of Purple		
⊿	= 3346	2	◈	= 550	1
O	= 3347	2	⊞	= 327	1
—	= 3345	1	≡	= 554	1
X	= 470	1			
II	= 471	1	Tints of Blue		
U	= 937	1	▨	= 823	1
◉	= 986	1	⊼	= 820	1
I	= 987	1	◐	= 798	1
V	= 988	1			
S	= 989	1	Tints of Red		
△	= 320	1	◿	= 3685	1
L	= 368	1	⊘	= 915	1
●	= 895	1	⚲	= 603	1
Φ	= 3012	1			

Tints of Brown

•	= 839	1
▨	= 841	1
▲	= 611	1
◗	= 611 (Holbein St.)	

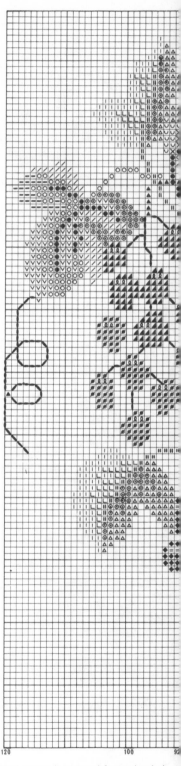

One-thread square is counted for each stitch.

Center

Center

Flower Garden Table Center, *shown on page 12.*

MATERIALS: White Oxford cloth (79 vertical and horizontal threads per 10cm square), 73cm by 47cm. D.M.C. 6-strand embroidery floss, No. 25: See Color Key for colors and amounts.

FINISHED SIZE: 66cm by 40cm.

DIRECTIONS: Find center of each border by folding fabric. Work in cross-stitch following chart. To finish, draw 4 threads on all sides, turn back 1cm and 2.5cm hem miter corners, and hem-stitch picking up 3 threads at a time (see page 109).

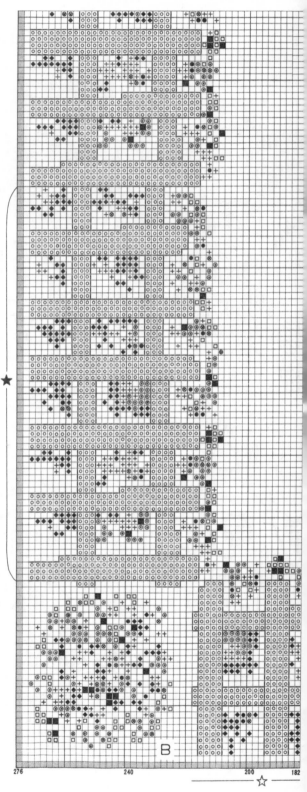

COLOR KEY

Use 3 strands of floss unless otherwise indicated.

Color No. Skeins

Tints of Green		Tints of Pink	
◈ = 320	2	■ = 604	0.5
□ = 369	2	⊗ = 605	0.5
◉ = 472	2		
+ = 704	2		

White ○		7
Ash gray □ = 414	(Use 2 strands & Holbein St.)	1
Plum ● = 554		1

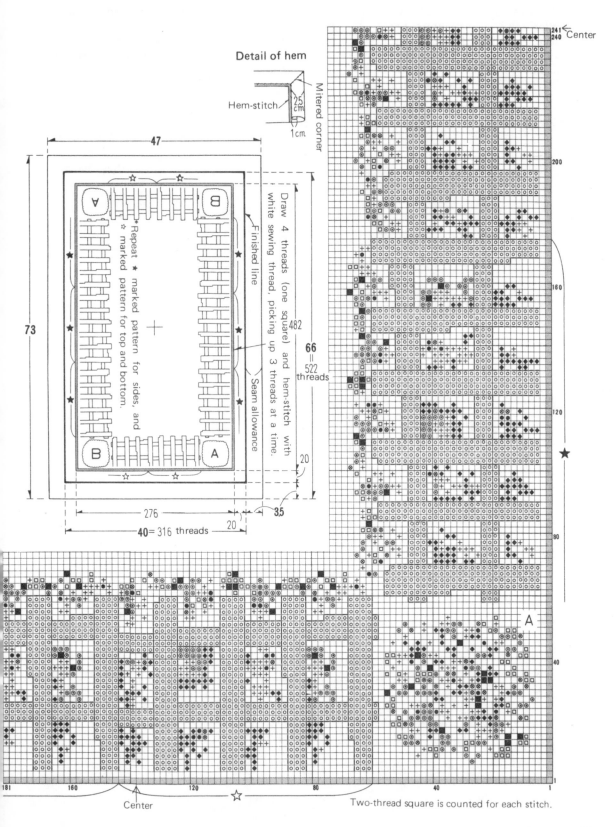

Detail of hem

Hem-stitch

Mitered corner

2.5 cm

1 cm

47

73

*Repeat ★ marked pattern for sides, and ☆ marked pattern for top and bottom.

Finished line

Seam allowance

Draw 4 threads (one square) and hem-stitch with white sewing thread, picking up 3 threads at a time.

482

66 = 522 threads

20

3.5

276

20

40 = 316 threads

241
240 ← Center

200

160

120

★

80

A

40

181   160   120   80   40   1

Center   ☆

Two-thread square is counted for each stitch.

Small Flower Table Runner, *shown on page 20*.

MATERIALS: Olive green Aida cloth (35 vertical and horizontal threads per 10cm square), 46cm by 112cm. D.M.C. 6-strand embroidery floss, No. 25: See Color Key for colors and amounts.
FINISHED SIZE: 105cm by 39cm.

DIRECTIONS: Decide embroidery area by counting threads of fabric. Work in cross-stitch, following chart. To finish, turn back 1cm and 2.5cm hem on all edges, miter corners and slip-stitch (see page 109).

Detail of hem

Design for border

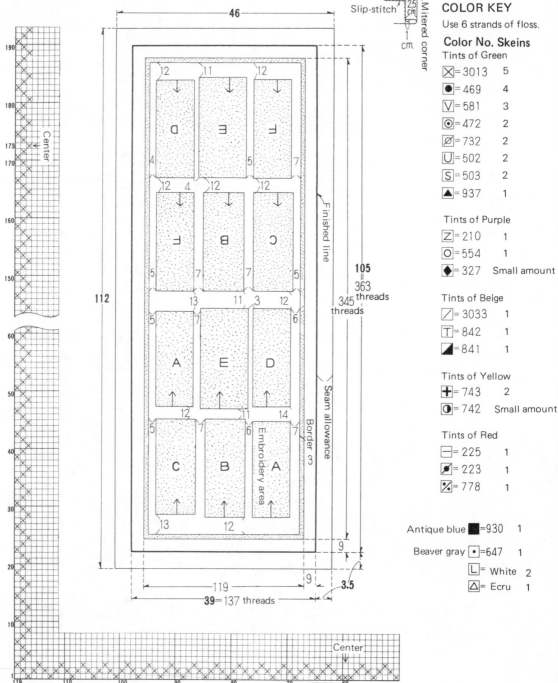

Slip-stitch

Mitered corner

2.5 cm

1 cm

COLOR KEY

Use 6 strands of floss.

Color No. Skeins

Tints of Green

X	= 3013	5
●	= 469	4
V	= 581	3
⊙	= 472	2
⊘	= 732	2
U	= 502	2
S	= 503	2
▲	= 937	1

Tints of Purple

Z	= 210	1
O	= 554	1
◆	= 327	Small amount

Tints of Beige

⁄	= 3033	1
T	= 842	1
◢	= 841	1

Tints of Yellow

+	= 743	2
◑	= 742	Small amount

Tints of Red

⊟	= 225	1
◪	= 223	1
⧄	= 778	1

Antique blue	■	= 930	1
Beaver gray	⊡	= 647	1
	L	= White	2
	△	= Ecru	1

One-thread square is counted for each stitch.

Street and Lampshade *Panels, shown on page 28.*

MATERIALS: Beige Oxford cloth (79 vertical and horizontal threads per 10cm square), 38cm by 29cm. D.M.C. 6-strand embroidery floss, No. 25: See Color Key for colors and amounts.

Street panel

Center Two-thread square is counted for each stitch.

21 = 160 threads

Color Key   Use 3 strands of floss.

Color No. Skeins

Tints of Gray		Tints of Blue					
U = 645	1	△ = 311	0.5	▲ = 310	0.5	◉ = 552 Small amount	⊟ = 3023 1
• = 646	0.5	T = 791	1	☐ = 310 (Holbein St.)		╱ = 727 0.5	
Ⅱ = 414	0.5	◑ = 931	1	● = 3371	1	☒ = 741 Small amount	

56

FINISHED SIZE: Street Panel, 27cm by 21cm. Lampshade Panel, 28cm by 21cm (embroidery area).

DIRECTIONS: Find center point of fabric and work in cross-stitch, following chart. Mount and frame.

Lampshade panel

28 = 220 threads → Center

Center Two-thread square is counted for each stitch.

21 = 160 threads

Color No. Skeins

COLOR KEY
Use 3 strands of floss.

Tints of Gray		Tints of Pink		Tints of Green						
◕=645	1	Ⅲ=603	0.5	◎=320	0.5	◑=931	0.5	Black ☐=310		
•=647	1	O=351	Small amount	△=3013	Small amount	T=680	0.5	(Holbein St.) Small amount		
✚=648	1	╱=761	1	S=993	" -	◉=741	Small amount	Beige ▲=840 "		
⊕=414	1	U=3688	1			━=677	0.5	brown		

57

Bedspread, *shown on page 8.*

MATERIALS: Beige Aida cloth (30 vertical and horizontal threads per 10cm square), 58cm by 281cm. Blue quilted velveteen, 92cm by 558cm. D.M.C. 6-strand embroidery floss, No. 25: See Color Key for colors and amounts on page 60. Blue cord for piping, 0.5cm by 558cm. Blue bias tape, 2.5cm by 935cm.
FINISHED SIZE: 275cm by 176cm.

DIRECTIONS: 1. Find center point of embroidery fabric and work in cross-stitch, following chart. 2. Cut quilted fabric as indicated. 3. Join quilted fabric together. Press seams open and slip-stitch each edge to wrong side of quilted fabric. 4. Place embroidered piece on center of quilted fabric and machine-stitch each side with corded piping in between. 5. Turn back all edges and sew on bias tape.

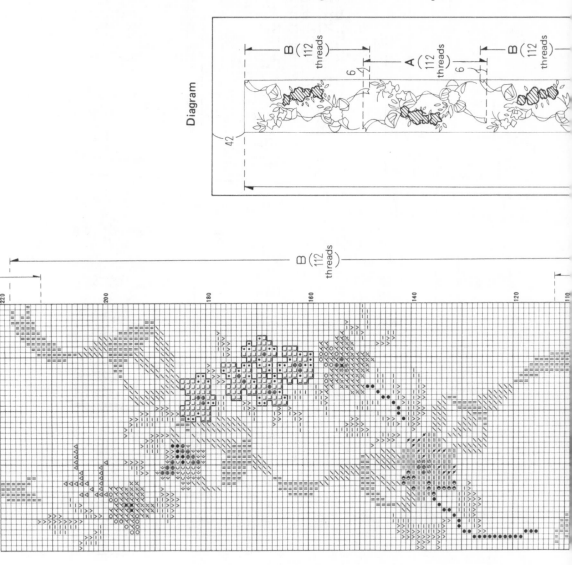

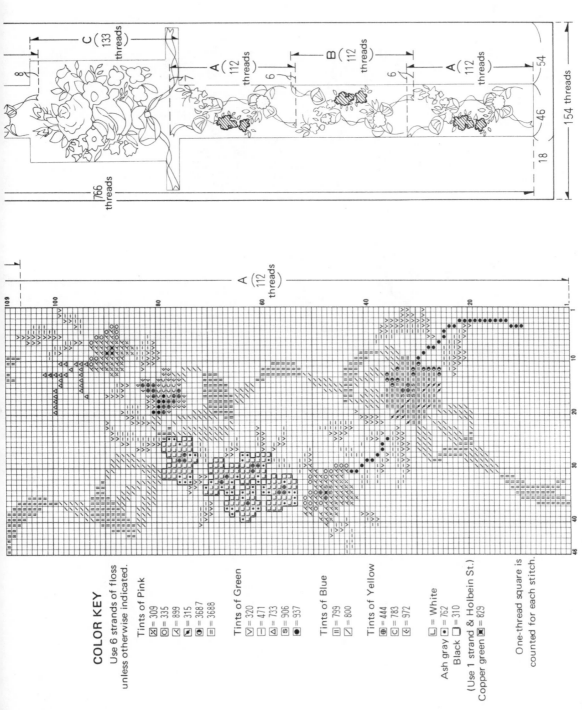

COLOR KEY

Use 6 strands of floss
unless otherwise indicated.

Tints of Pink
⊠ = 309
◎ = 335
⊠ = 899
◣ = 315
◉ = 3687
▤ = 3688

Tints of Green
▽ = 320
▯ = 471
△ = 733
S = 906
◉ = 937

Tints of Blue
▥ = 799
◿ = 800

Tints of Yellow
⊕ = 444
C = 783
◁ = 972

☐ = White
● = 762
Ash gray ☐ = 310
Black
(Use 1 strand & Holbein St.)
Copper green ⊠ = 829

One-thread square is
counted for each stitch.

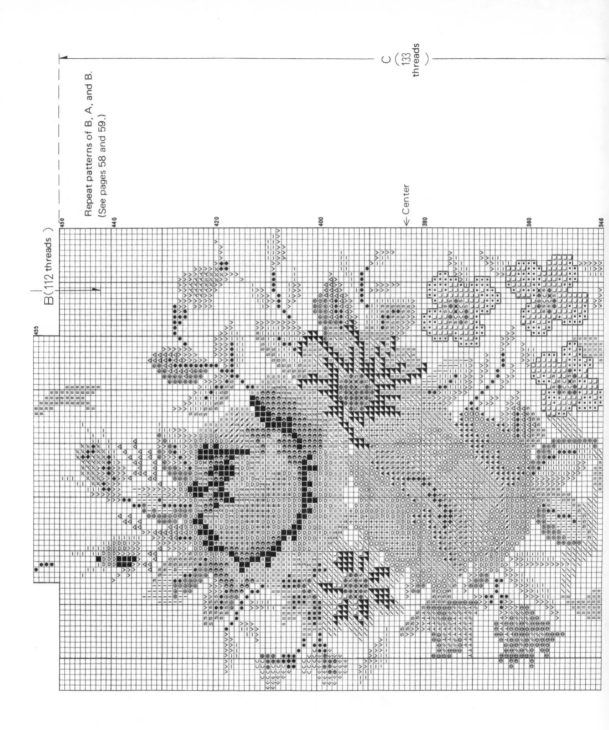

Repeat patterns of B, A, and B.
(See pages 58 and 59.)

B (112 threads)

C (133 threads)

← Center

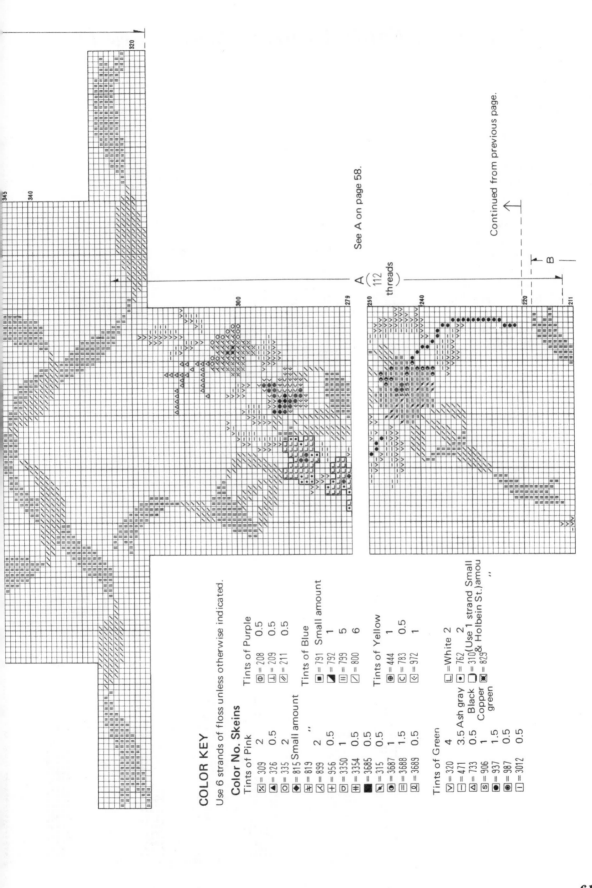

COLOR KEY

Use 6 strands of floss unless otherwise indicated.

Color No. Skeins

Tints of Pink

⊠ = 309	2	
◀ = 326	0.5	
⊙ = 335	2	
◈ = 815	Small amount	
⊞ = 819	2	"
⊠ = 899	0.5	
⊞ = 956	1	
⊡ = 3350	0.5	
⊞ = 3354	0.5	
■ = 3685	0.5	
⊘ = 315	0.5	
⊟ = 3687	1	
⊟ = 3688	1.5	
⊠ = 3689	0.5	

Tints of Purple

⊕ = 208	0.5
⊥ = 209	0.5
⊘ = 211	0.5

Tints of Blue

■ = 791	Small amount
◣ = 792	1
⊟ = 799	5
⊘ = 800	6

Tints of Yellow

⊕ = 444	1
C = 783	0.5
⊡ = 972	1

Tints of Green

⊻ = 320	4
⊡ = 471	3.5 Ash gray
◣ = 733	0.5 Black
S = 906	1 Copper
◉ = 937	1.5 green
⊙ = 987	0.5
⊡ = 3012	0.5

☐ = White 2
● = 762 2
☐ = 310 (Use 1 strand Small
⊠ = 829 & Holbein St.)amou
          "

See A on page 58.

Continued from previous page.

A (112 threads)

61

Narcissus Table Center, *shown on page 13.*

MATERIALS: Beige Indian cloth (52 vertical and horizontal threads per 10cm square), 88cm by 46cm. D.M.C. 6-strand embroidery floss, No. 25: See Color Key for colors and amounts.

FINISHED SIZE: 40cm by 82cm.

DIRECTIONS: Find center of top and bottom sides and work in cross-stitch, following chart. To finish, turn back 1cm and 2cm hem on all edges, miter corners and slip-stitch (see page 109).

COLOR KEY

Use 4 strands of floss unless otherwise indicated.

Color No. Skeins

Tints of Green

Ⓞ	= 368	2
⏺	= 987	3
◉	= 988	4
✕	= 989	7.5
⌐⌐	= 989 (Use 2 strands & Holbein St.)	
Ⓤ	= 3348	1

Tints of Yellow

▲	= 725	1
Ⓞ	= 744	1
Ⓛ	= 3078	1

╱	= White	6
Ash gray ✚	= 415	1

187   160   140   120   108

46

88

Detail of hem

2cm

1 cm | Slip-stitch

Mitered corner

Finished line

Seam allowance

93

403

82 = 423 threads

155

10

187

40 = 207 threads

10

3

Center

107   100   80   60   40   20   1

155

140

120

100

80

60

40

20

1

Wild Flower Pillow, shown on page 7.

MATERIALS: Beige Aida cloth (41 vertical and horizontal threads per 10cm square), 91cm by 57cm. D.M.C. 6-strand embroidery floss, No. 25: See Color Key for colors and amounts. Inner pillow, 45cm by 55cm, stuffed with 500g kapok. 42cm-long zipper.

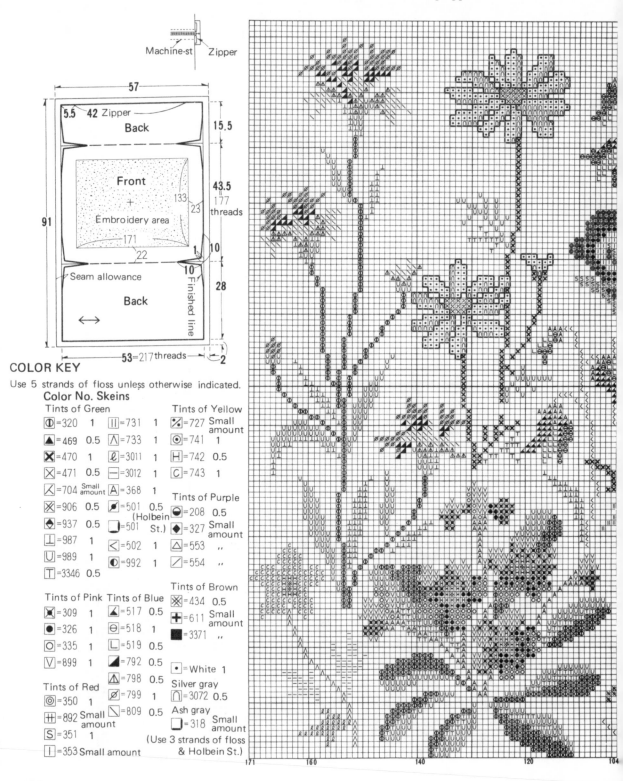

COLOR KEY

Use 5 strands of floss unless otherwise indicated.

Color No. Skeins

Tints of Green

⏀=320	1	‖‖=731	1
▲=469	0.5	⋀=733	1
✖=470	1	ℓ=3011	1
✕=471	0.5	−=3012	1
⋋=704 Small amount		A=368	1
⊠=906	0.5		
◆=937	0.5		
⊥=987	1		
U=989	1		
T=3346	0.5		

Tints of Pink

✖=309	1
●=326	1
O=335	1
V=899	1

Tints of Red

◎=350	1
⊞=892 Small amount	
S=351	1
I=353 Small amount	

Tints of Blue

▲=517	0.5
⊖=518	1
L=519	0.5
◢=792	0.5
⊿=798	0.5
∅=799	1
◥=809	0.5

Tints of Yellow

⁒=727 Small amount	
⊙=741	1
H=742	0.5
C=743	1

Tints of Purple

⊝=208	0.5
◆=327 Small amount	
△=553	,,
◿=554	,,

Tints of Brown

⊠=434	0.5
✚=611 Small amount	
■=3371	,,

◽∙=White 1

Silver gray
∩=3072 0.5

Ash gray
⬚=318 Small amount
(Use 3 strands of floss & Holbein St.)

✎=501 0.5 (Holbein St.)
⬚=501 St.)
◁=502 1
◖=992 1

64

FINISHED SIZE: 43.5cm by 53cm.
DIRECTIONS: 1. Find center point of FRONT piece and work in cross-stitch, following chart. 2. Sew ends of BACK pieces together (5.5cm) and sew on zipper. 3. With right sides facing, stitch along seam lines. Turn to right side. Insert inner pillow.

← Center

One-thread square is counted for each stitch.

Center

Coasters, *shown on page 14.*

MATERIALS FOR ONE COASTER: Beige linen (130 vertical and horizontal threads per 10cm square), 14cm by 14cm square. D.M.C. 6-strand embroidery floss, No. 25: See Color Key for colors and amounts.

FINISHED SIZE: 11cm by 11cm square.

DIRECTIONS: Work in cross-stitch, following the chart. Turn back 0.5cm and 1cm hem on all edges, miter corners and slip-stitch (see page 109).

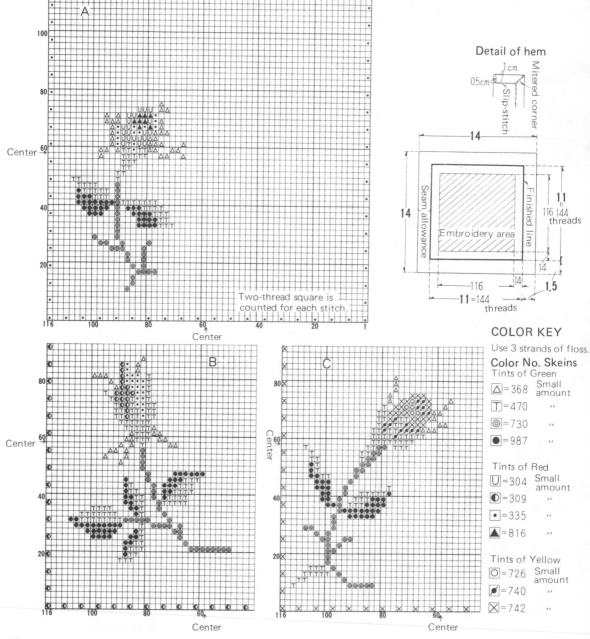

Two-thread square is counted for each stitch.

Detail of hem

1cm
0.5cm
Mitered corner
Slip-stitch

Seam allowance
Finished line
Embroidery area

14
14

14

11 144 threads
14
1.5

116
14
11 = 144 threads

COLOR KEY

Use 3 strands of floss.

Color No. Skeins

Tints of Green

△ = 368	Small amount	
T = 470	"	
◎ = 730	"	
● = 987	"	

Tints of Red

U = 304	Small amount	
◐ = 309	"	
• = 335	"	
▲ = 816	"	

Tints of Yellow

O = 726	Small amount	
⌀ = 740	"	
X = 742	"	

Octagon Doily, *shown on page 25.*

MATERIALS: Yellow Indian cloth (52 vertical and horizontal threads per 10cm square), 37cm by 37cm square. D.M.C. 6-strand embroidery floss, No. 25: See Color Key for colors and amounts.

FINISHED SIZE: See diagram.
DIRECTIONS: Find center point of fabric and select embroidery area. Work in cross-stitch, following chart. Turn back all edges and slipstitch.

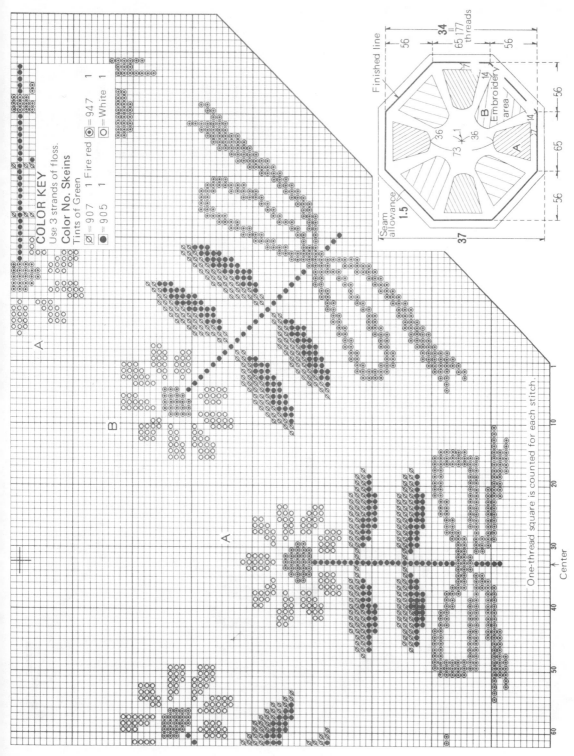

COLOR KEY
Use 3 strands of floss.
Color No. Skeins
Tints of Green
⊘ = 907   1   Fire red ◉ = 947   1
● = 905   1   ○ = White   1

One-thread square is counted for each stitch.

Piano Cover, shown on page 19.

MATERIALS: Beige Aida cloth (35 vertical and horizontal threads per 10cm square), 85cm by 200cm. D.M.C. 6-strand embroidery floss, No. 25: See Color Key for colors and amounts.
FINISHED SIZE: 76cm by 191cm.
DIRECTIONS: Decide on embroidery area by counting threads of fabric. Work in cross-stitch, following chart. To finish, turn back 1.5cm and 3cm hem on all edges, miter corners and slip-stitch (see page 109).

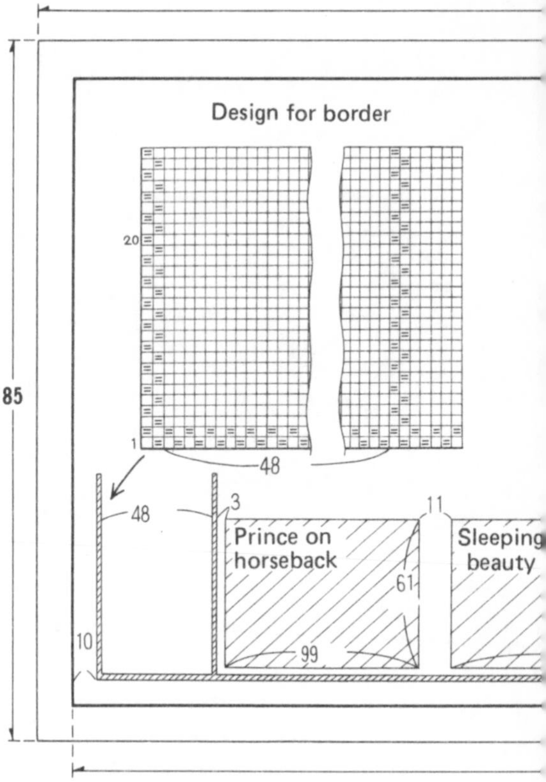

Design for border
20
1
48
48
3
11
Prince on horseback
Sleeping beauty
61
10
99
85

COLOR KEY

Use 6 strands of floss.

Color No.	Skeins
Tints of Blue	
☰=792	4
⧄=793	2
L=794	1
◎=797	1
S=828	1
Tints of Purple	
⊠=3041	1
+=3042	1
Tints of Pink	
Φ=776	1
Z=899	1
●=3328	1
O=3688	4
Tints of Gray	
I=318	3
■=413	4
◆=645	2
−=762	1
V=3072	1
Tints of Green	
E=3052	1
/=3053	4
Tints of Brown	
∀=642	2
□=950	1
6=780	1
Saffron	
△=725	1
•=White	2

One-thread square is counted for each stitch.

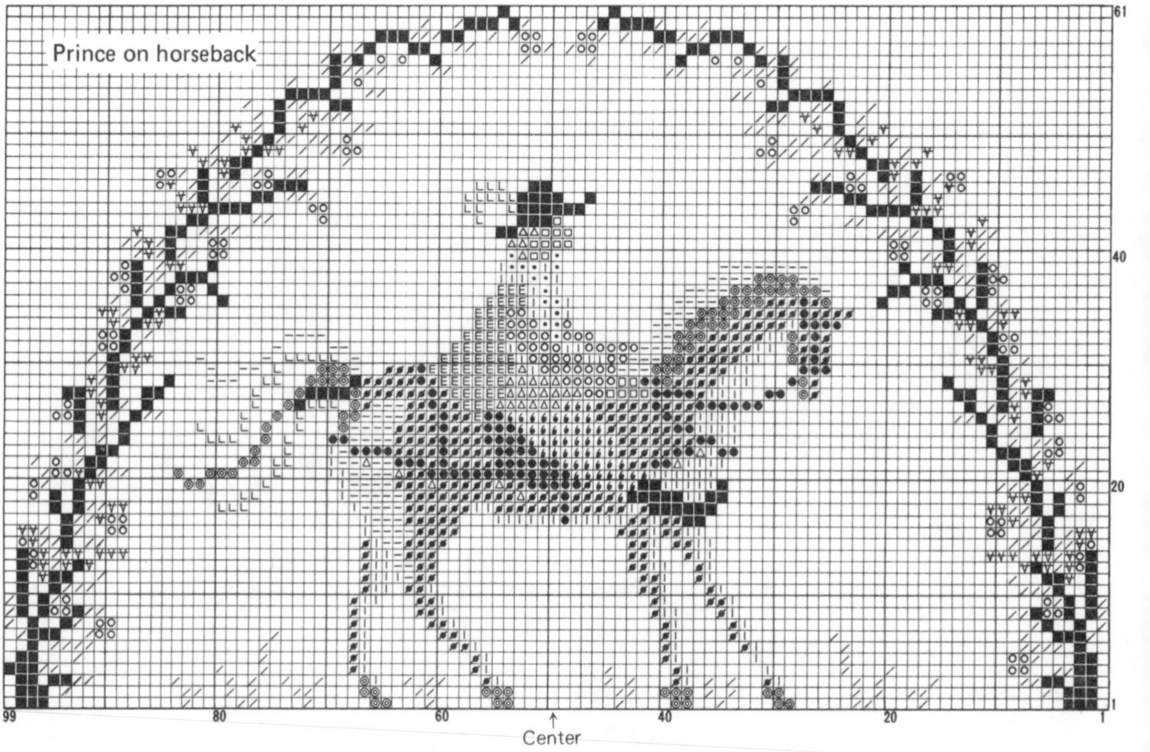

Prince on horseback
61
40
20
1
99
80
60
40
20
1
Center

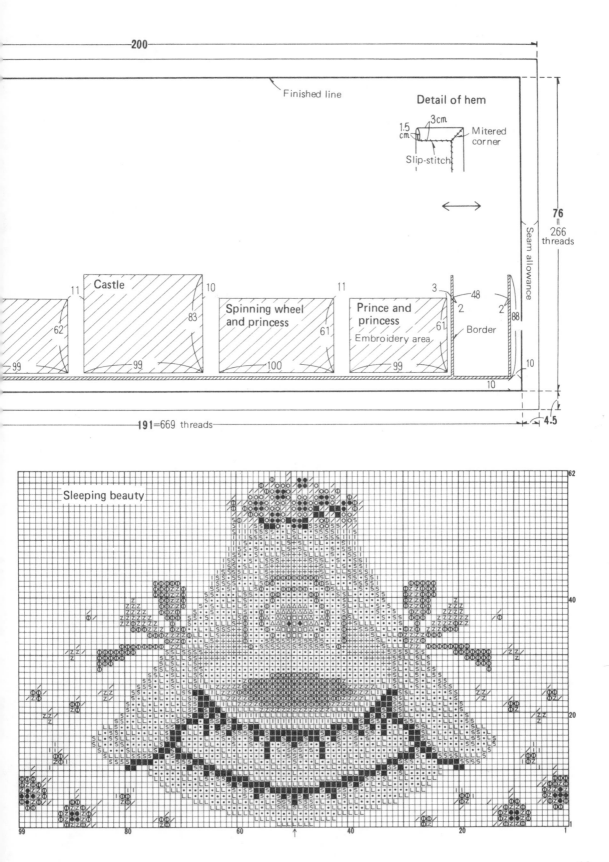

200

Finished line

Detail of hem

3cm
1.5 cm
Mitered corner
Slip-stitch

76 = 266 threads

Seam allowance

Castle
11
10
62
83
99
99

Spinning wheel and princess
11
61
100

Prince and princess
Embroidery area
3
61
99

48
2
Border

2
88

10

10

4.5

191 = 669 threads

Sleeping beauty

62

40

20

99   80   60   40   20   1

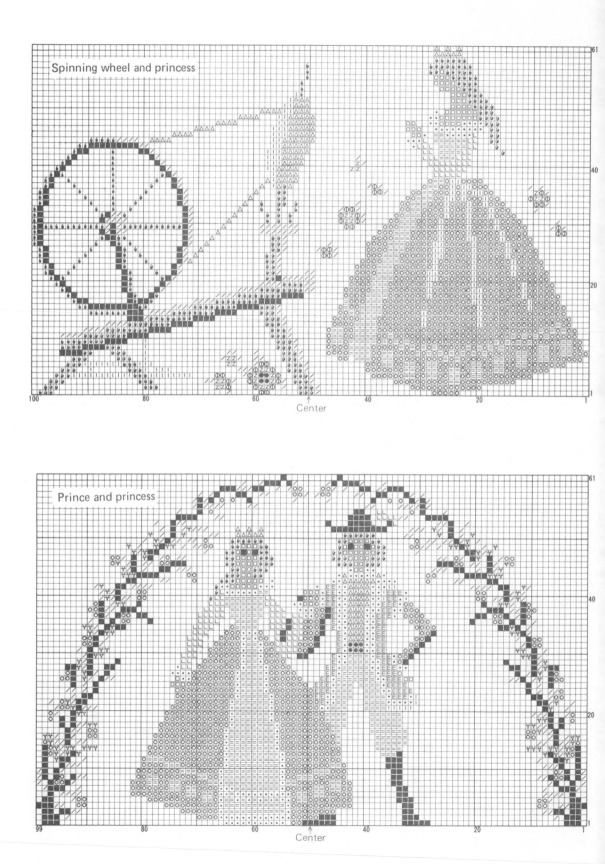

Spinning wheel and princess

Prince and princess

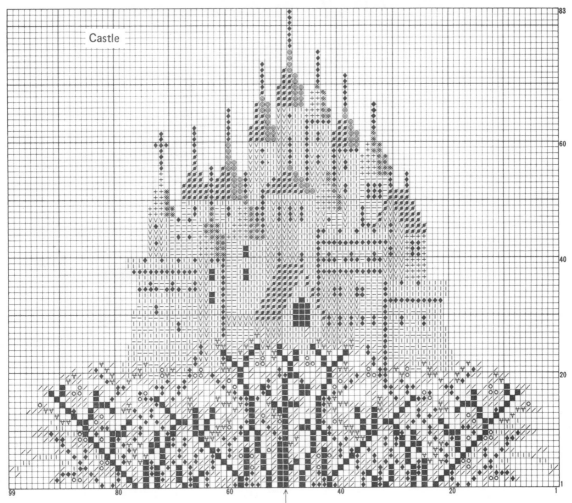

Castle

Center of design

Castle Panel, *shown on page 18.*

MATERIALS: Beige Aida cloth (35 vertical and horizontal threads per 10cm square), 52.5cm by 45.5cm. D.M.C. 6-strand embroidery floss, No. 25: See Color Key for colors and amounts.
FINISHED SIZE: 24cm by 28.5cm (embroidery area).
DIRECTIONS: Same design as Castle of Piano Cover is used. Find center point of fabric and work in cross-stitch, following chart. Mount and frame.

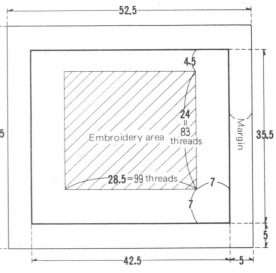

Oval Doily, *shown on page 24.*

COLOR KEY Use 3 strands of floss.
Color No. Skeins

Tints of Green Tints of Red-brown

T = 469 0.5	⊙ = 355 Small amount
⊞ = 470 Small amount	⋈ = 743 Small amount
∨ = 356 0.5	Tangerine yellow
● = 935 1	▲ = 3046 Beige
◨ = 937 0.5	∅ = 758 Small amount
‖ = 319 Small amount	□ = 3078 Light yellow 0.5
□ = 368 "	⊞ = White 0.5
○ = 369 "	

One-thread square is counted for each stitch.

MATERIALS: Olive green Indian cloth (52 vertical and horizontal threads per 10cm square), 44cm by 34cm. D.M.C. 6-strand embroidery floss, No. 25: See Color Key for colors and amounts. Olive green crochet cotton (No. 6 crochet hook). Bias tape, 1.2cm by 120cm.
FINISHED SIZE: See diagram.
DIRECTIONS: Find center point and select embroidery area. Work in cross-stitch, following chart. Turn back 2cm hem and sew on bias tape. Crochet edging and sew it all around.

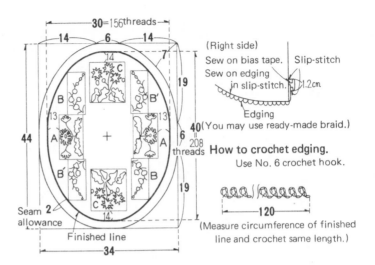

(Right side)
Sew on bias tape. | Slip-stitch
Sew on edging in slip-stitch. 1.2cm
Edging
(You may use ready-made braid.)
How to crochet edging.
Use No. 6 crochet hook.
120
(Measure circumference of finished line and crochet same length.)

Bedspread, shown on page 17.

MATERIALS: Beige Aida cloth (30 vertical and horizontal threads per 10cm square), 85cm by 540cm. Purple heavy-weight cotton broadcloth, 92cm by 852cm. D.M.C. Embroidery cotton (Coton à broder): See Color Key for colors and amounts.
FINISHED SIZE: 280cm by 176cm.
DIRECTIONS: 1. Cut fabrics.
2. Sew two pieces of Aida cloth together and press seam open.

3. Find center point of joined piece and select embroidery area. Work in cross-stitch, following chart.
4. Sew two pieces of lining together.
5. Sew border strips to embroidered fabric and miter corners.
6. With right sides of embroidered fabric and lining together, stitch four sides, leaving opening. Turn to right side. Slip-stitch opening closed.
7. Machine-stitch along the edge.

Detail of joining

Diagram
Add 2cm seam allowance.

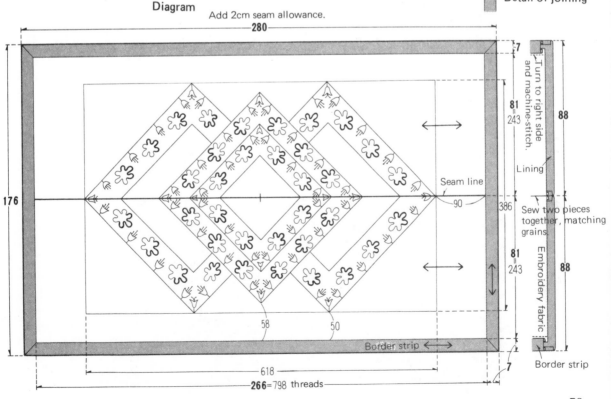

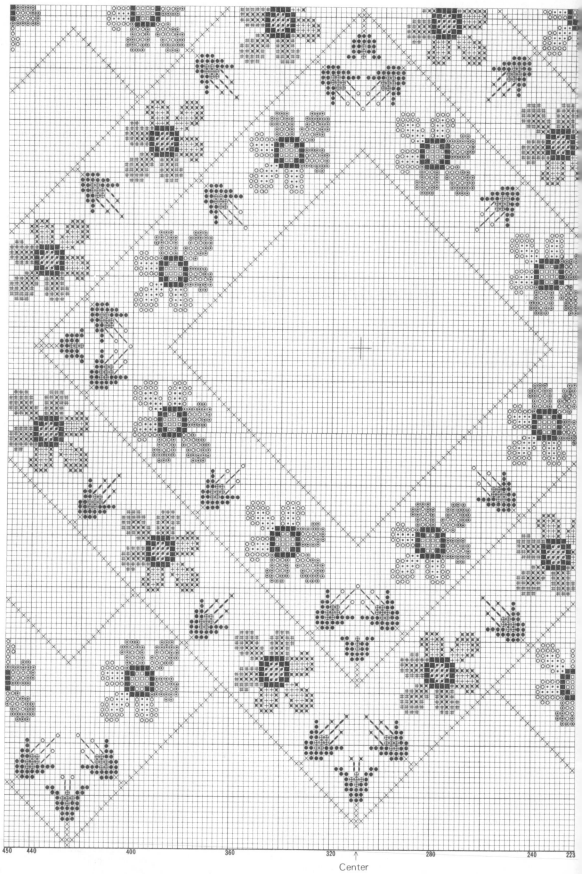

450   440   400   360   320   280   240   223

Center

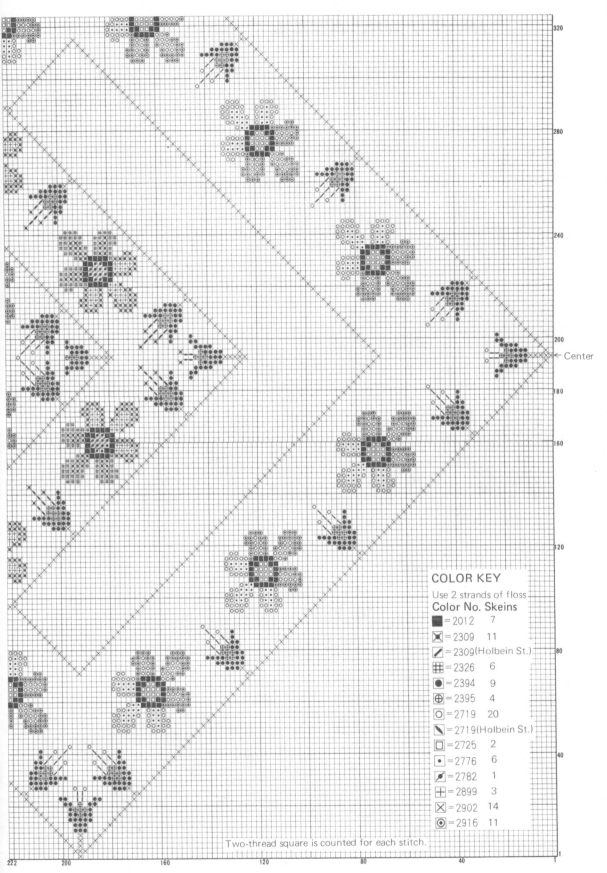

320

280

240

200 ← Center

180

160

120

COLOR KEY

Use 2 strands of floss
Color No. Skeins

■	= 2012	7
✕	= 2309	11
╱	= 2309(Holbein St.)	
⊞	= 2326	6
⬤	= 2394	9
⊕	= 2395	4
O	= 2719	20
◣	= 2719(Holbein St.)	
▢	= 2725	2
•	= 2776	6
◪	= 2782	1
✚	= 2899	3
✕	= 2902	14
◉	= 2916	11

80

40

1

Two-thread square is counted for each stitch.

222   200   160   120   80   40   1

Violet Table Runner, *shown on page 21.*

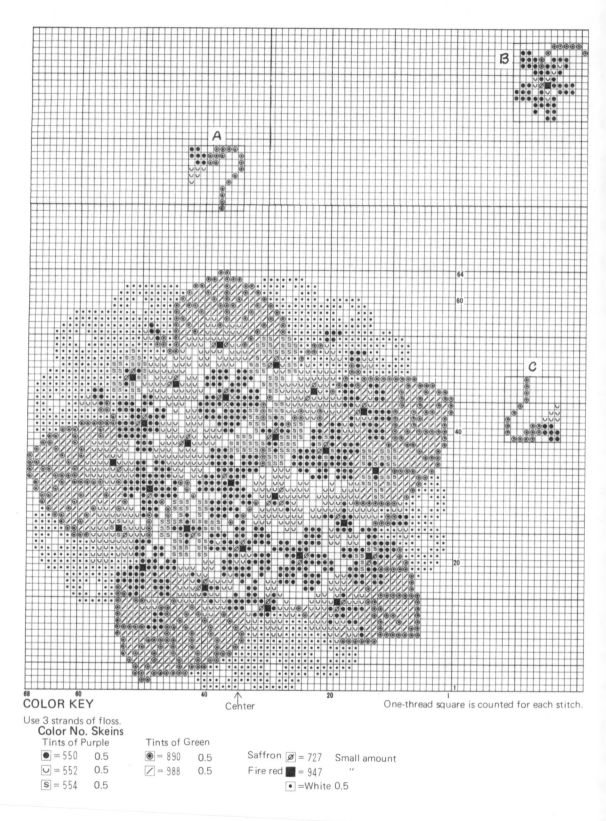

One-thread square is counted for each stitch.

COLOR KEY

Use 3 strands of floss.
Color No. Skeins

Tints of Purple		Tints of Green	
● = 550	0.5	◉ = 890	0.5
U = 552	0.5	╱ = 988	0.5
S = 554	0.5		

Saffron ∅ = 727 Small amount

Fire red ■ = 947 "

● =White 0.5

MATERIALS: Rose pink Aida cloth (41 vertical and horizontal threads per 10cm square), 74cm by 36.5cm. D.M.C. 6-strand embroidery floss, No. 25: See Color Key for colors and amounts. FINISHED SIZE: 31.5cm by 69cm.

DIRECTIONS: Select embroidery areas by counting threads of fabric. Work in cross-stitch, following chart. To finish, turn back 1cm and 1.5cm hem on all edges, miter corners and slip-stitch (see page 109).

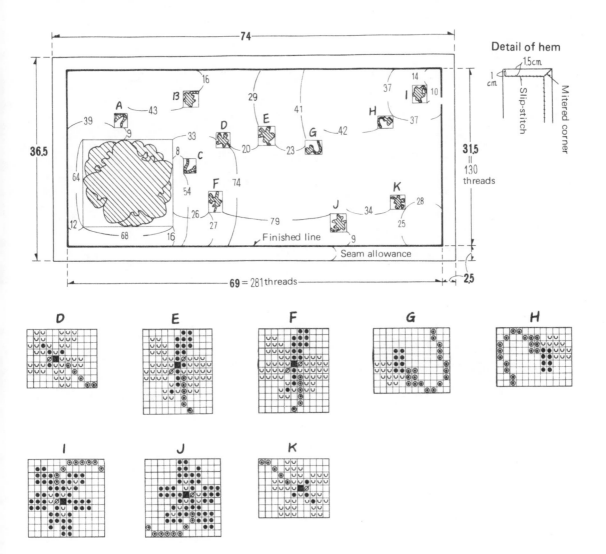

Cattleya Album, *shown on page 31.*

MATERIALS: Olive green Aida cloth (35 vertical and horizontal threads per 10cm square), 46cm by 94cm. D.M.C. 6-strand embroidery floss, No. 25: See Color Key for colors and amounts.

FINISHED SIZE: 36cm by 40cm.
DIRECTIONS: Select embroidery area by counting threads of fabric. Work in cross-stitch, following chart. You may need a professional's help to finish album.

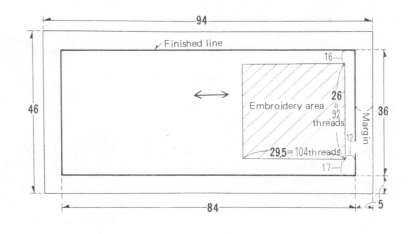

The finished line diagram shows: overall width 94, height 46, margin 5. Finished area 84 wide, 36 tall. Embroidery area: 26 (width), 92 threads (II), 29.5 = 104 threads, with markings 16, 12, 17, and "Margin".

Labels in diagram: Finished line, Embroidery area, Margin.

COLOR KEY

Use 6 strands of floss.

Color No. Skeins

Tints of Green		Tints of Red	
II = 469	0.5	● = 309	1
X = 470	0.5	∓ = 335	0.5
∧ = 471	0.5	V = 776	1
s = 937	1	— = 818	0.5
6 = 3345	1	O = 961	0.5
⊕ = 3346	1	I = 962	0.5
# = 3347	1	◹ = 3326	1
		⊥ = 3350	Small amount
		◪ = 3685	0.5

Tints of Purple		
◉ = 209	1	
△ = 210	1	
◎ = 211	1	
◼ = 552	Small amount	
■ = 553	1	
U = 554	0.5	
e = 718	0.5	
◐ = 915	0.5	
L = 917	0.5	

Tints of Yellow	
⊠ = 725	0.5
≡ = 726	0.5
+ = 727	0.5
⊠ = 741	Small amount
⊘ = 745	0.5
■ = 780	Small amount
◆ = 783	0.5

● = White   1

One-thread square is counted for each stitch.

←Center

Christmas Wall Hanging, *shown on page 26.*

MATERIALS: Beige Oxford cloth (79 vertical and horizontal threads per 10cm square), 46.5cm by 43cm. D.M.C. 6-strand embroidery floss, No. 25: See Color Key for colors and amounts. Golden cord for hanging, 40cm long. Wooden dowel, 0.6cm in diameter and 19cm long. One big golden bell. Two small bells.

FINISHED SIZE: 41cm by 16cm.

DIRECTIONS: Work in cross-stitch, following chart. Make up for wall hanging, following directions on next page. Attach bells in place.

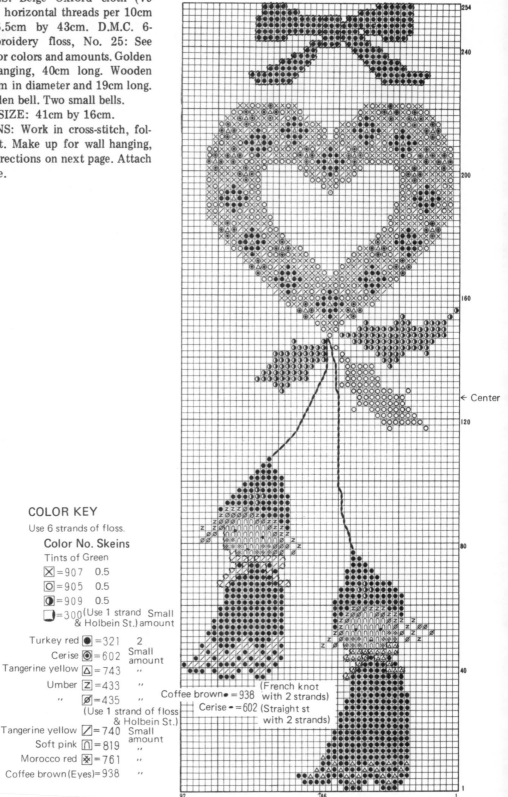

← Center

COLOR KEY

Use 6 strands of floss.

Color No. Skeins

Tints of Green

☒	= 907	0.5
⦿	= 905	0.5
◑	= 909	0.5
▭	= 300	(Use 1 strand Small & Holbein St.) amount

Turkey red	●	= 321	2
Cerise	◉	= 602	Small amount
Tangerine yellow	△	= 743	ʺ
Umber	Z	= 433	ʺ
ʺ	⌀	= 435	ʺ

(Use 1 strand of floss & Holbein St.)

Tangerine yellow	⧄	= 740	Small amount
Soft pink	⋒	= 819	ʺ
Morocco red	✳	= 761	ʺ
Coffee brown (Eyes)	= 938	ʺ

Coffee brown ● = 938 (French knot with 2 strands)

Cerise ▬ = 602 (Straight st with 2 strands)

Two-thread square is counted for each stitch. — Center

80

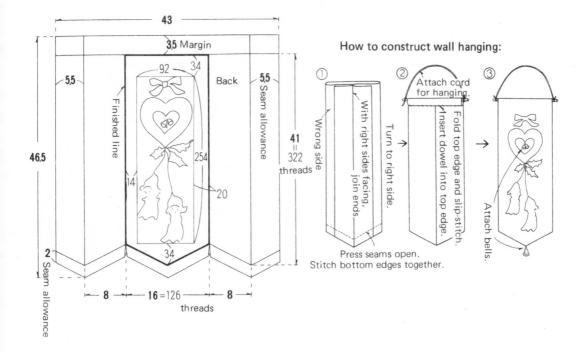

Fruit Wall Hanging, *shown on page 26.*

MATERIALS: Natural-colored Indian cloth (52 vertical and horizontal threads per 10cm square), 63cm by 25cm. D.M.C. 6-strand embroidery floss, No. 25: See Color Key for colors and amounts. One pair of hanging attachments. Adhesive interlining, 53cm by 10cm.

FINISHED SIZE: 53 cm by 10 cm.

DIRECTIONS: Select embroidery areas by counting threads of fabric. Work in cross-stitch, following chart. Place adhesive interlining on wrong side of embroidered fabric and press. Join ends and bring seams to center. Turn to right side. Place hanging attachments at top and bottom. Turn back top and bottom hems as shown and slip-stitch.

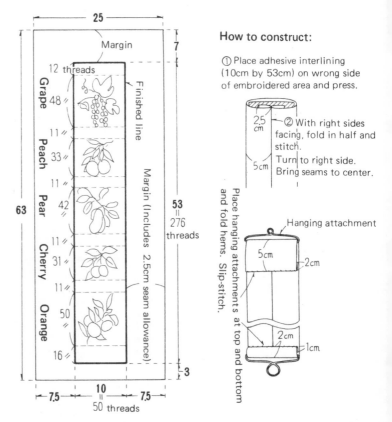

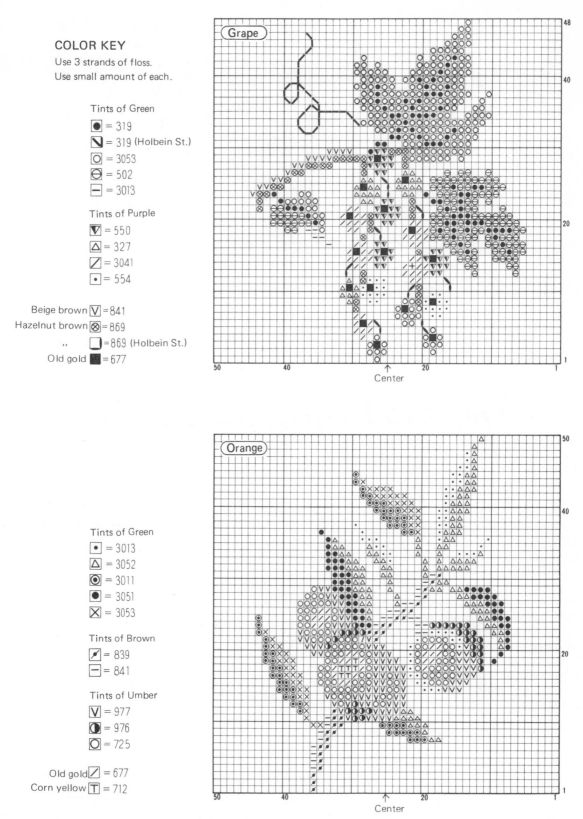

COLOR KEY

Use 3 strands of floss.
Use small amount of each.

Tints of Green

- ● = 319
- ◣ = 319 (Holbein St.)
- ○ = 3053
- ⊖ = 502
- – = 3013

Tints of Purple

- ▼ = 550
- △ = 327
- / = 3041
- · = 554

Beige brown V = 841
Hazelnut brown ⊗ = 869
"] = 869 (Holbein St.)
Old gold ■ = 677

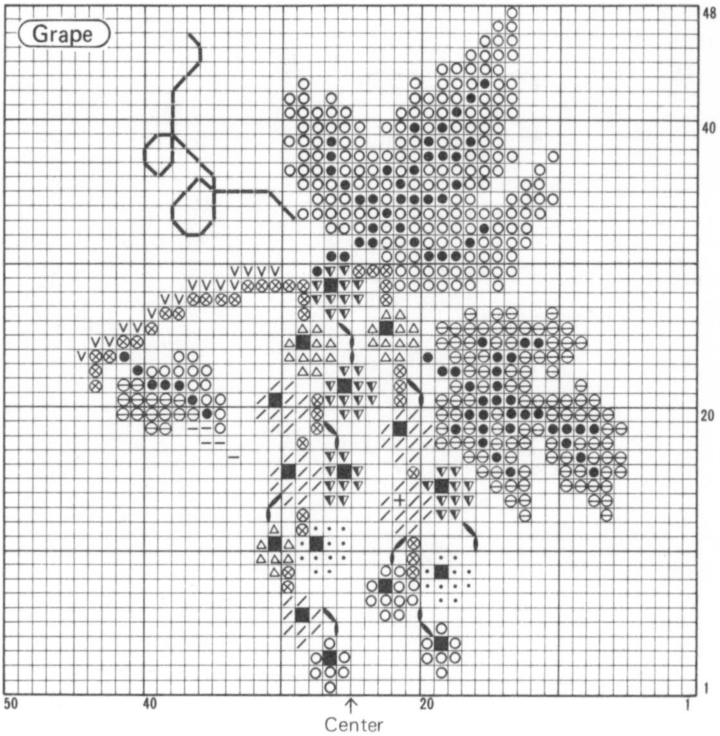

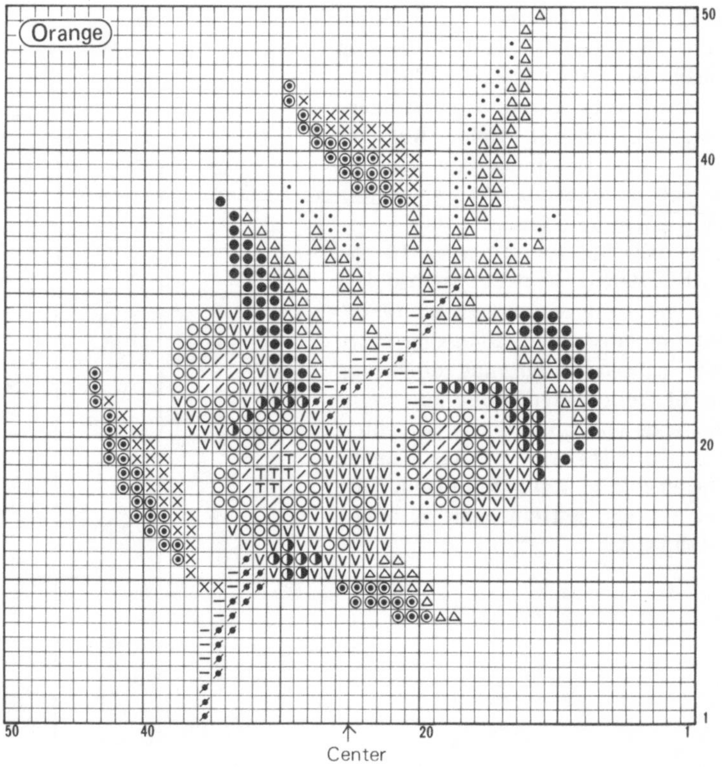

Tints of Green

- · = 3013
- △ = 3052
- ⦿ = 3011
- ● = 3051
- ✕ = 3053

Tints of Brown

- ⁄ = 839
- – = 841

Tints of Umber

- V = 977
- ◐ = 976
- ○ = 725

Old gold / = 677
Corn yellow T = 712

One-thread square is counted for each stitch.

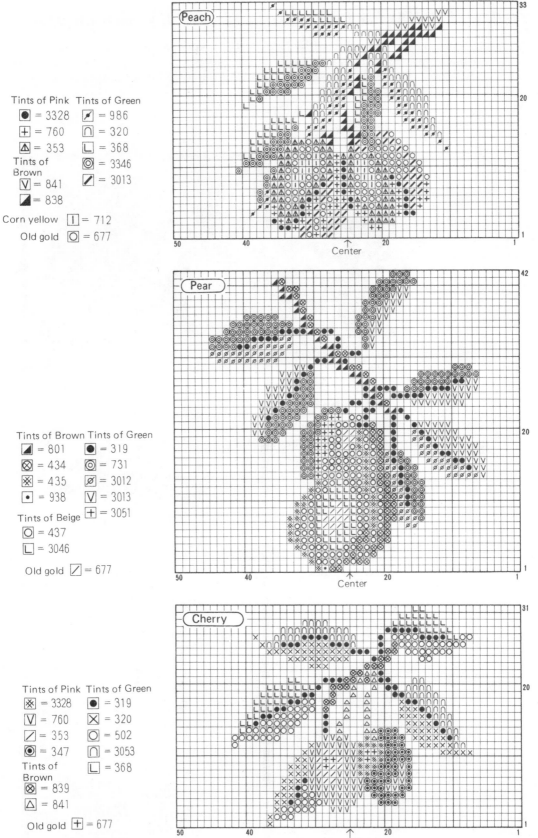

Peach

Tints of Pink
● = 3328
✛ = 760
△ = 353

Tints of Brown
V = 841
◣ = 838

Corn yellow I = 712

Old gold ◎ = 677

Tints of Green
⟋ = 986
∩ = 320
L = 368
◎ = 3346
╱ = 3013

Pear

Tints of Brown
◢ = 801
⊗ = 434
⊠ = 435
⊡ = 938

Tints of Beige
○ = 437
L = 3046

Old gold ╱ = 677

Tints of Green
● = 319
◎ = 731
∅ = 3012
V = 3013
✛ = 3051

Cherry

Tints of Pink
⊠ = 3328
V = 760
╱ = 353
◉ = 347

Tints of Brown
⊗ = 839
△ = 841

Old gold ✛ = 677

Tints of Green
● = 319
X = 320
○ = 502
∩ = 3053
L = 368

83

Square Doily (Tree and House), *shown on page 25.*

MATERIALS: White Indian cloth (52 vertical and horizontal threads per 10cm square), 40cm by 40cm square. D.M.C. 6-strand embroidery floss, No. 25: See Color Key for colors and amounts.

FINISHED SIZE: 35cm by 35cm square.
DIRECTIONS: Select embroidery area by counting threads. Work in cross-stitch, following chart. Turn back hem on all edges and slip-stitch.

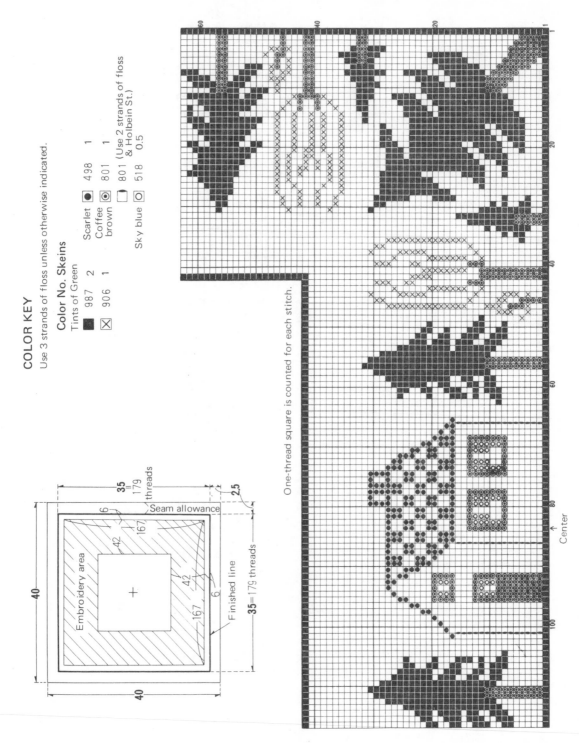

COLOR KEY
Use 3 strands of floss unless otherwise indicated.

Color No. Skeins
Tints of Green
- ■ 987 2
- ☒ 906 1

Scarlet ● 498 1
Coffee brown ◉ 801 1
801 (Use 2 strands of floss & Holbein St.)
Sky blue ◎ 518 0.5

One-thread square is counted for each stitch.

Table Runner and Placemats,

shown on pages 10 and 11.

FOR TABLE RUNNER:
MATERIALS: Beige linen (130 vertical and horizontal threads per 10cm square), 36.5cm by 119cm. D.M.C. 6-strand embroidery floss, No. 25: See Color Key for colors and amounts.
FINISHED SIZE: 112cm by 29.5cm.

DIRECTIONS: Select embroidery areas by counting threads of fabric. Work in cross-stitch, following chart. Draw two threads from fabric, turn back 1cm and 2.5cm hem on all edges, miter corners and hem-stitch (see page 109). **(Chart is shown on pages 86 and 87.)**

FOR PLACEMATS:
MATERIALS FOR 4 PLACEMATS: Beige linen (130 vertical and horizontal threads per 10cm square), 90cm by 68cm. D. M. C. 6-strand embroidery floss, No. 25: See Color Key for colors and amounts.
FINISHED SIZE: 27cm by 38cm.
DIRECTIONS: Select embroidery area by counting threads. Work in cross-stitch, following chart. Draw two threads from fabric, turn back 1cm and 2.5cm hem on all edges, miter corners and hem-stitch (see page 109).
(Charts are shown on pages 88 and 89.)

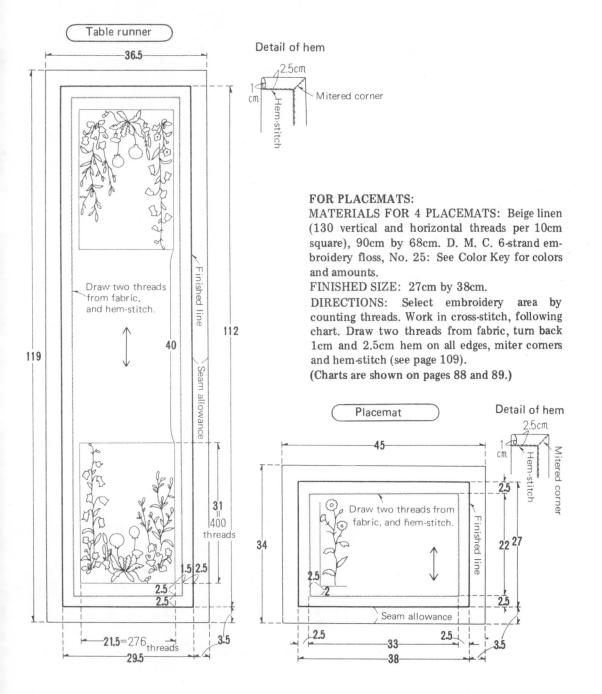

Table runner

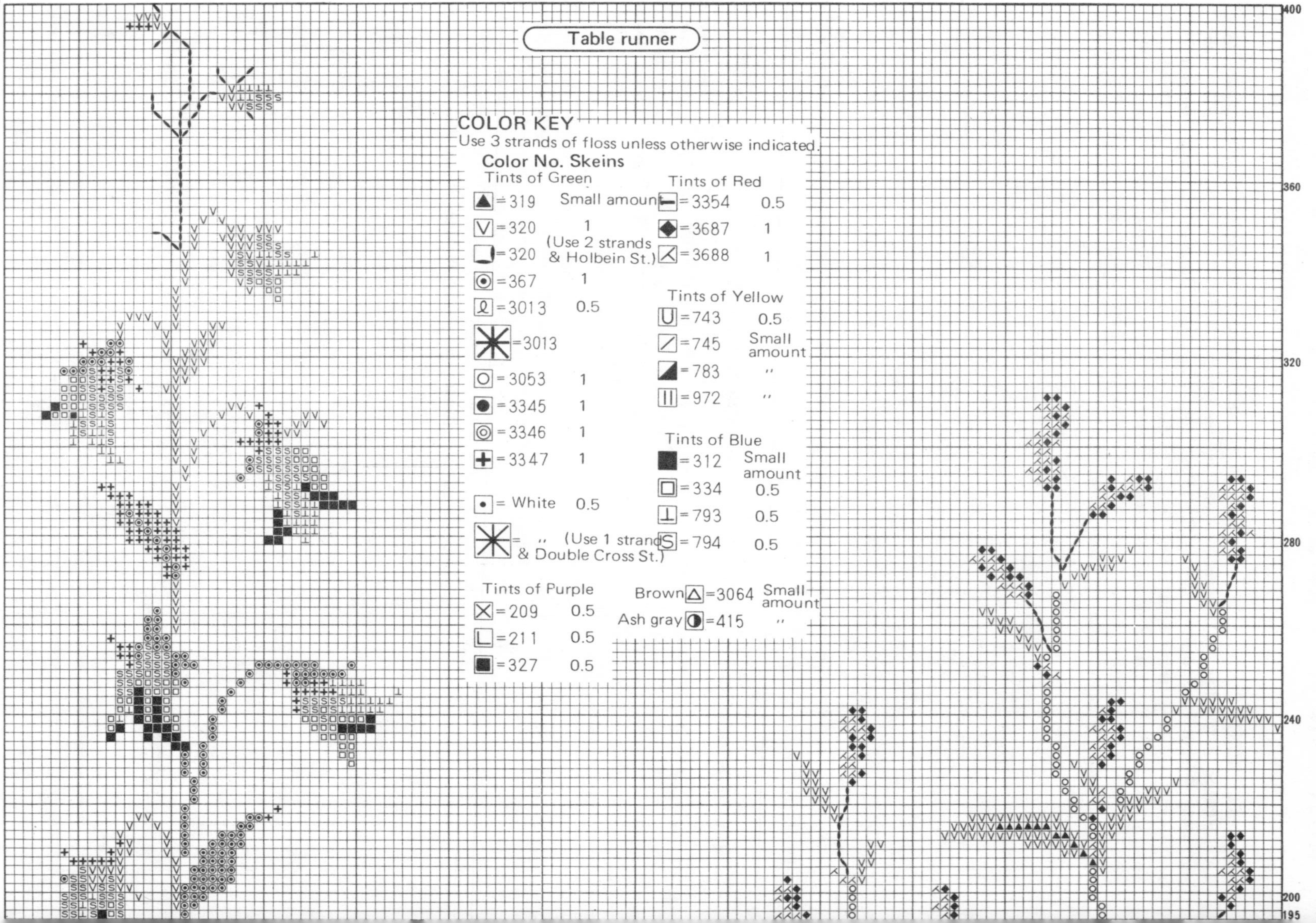

COLOR KEY

Use 3 strands of floss unless otherwise indicated.

Color No. Skeins

Symbol	Color No.	Skeins
Tints of Green		
▲	319	Small amount
V	320	1
❙ (Use 2 strands & Holbein St.)	320	
⊙	367	1
ℓ	3013	0.5
✳	3013	
○	3053	1
●	3345	1
◎	3346	1
✚	3347	1
•	White	0.5
✳ (Use 1 strand & Double Cross St.)	″	
Tints of Purple		
☒	209	0.5
L	211	0.5
■	327	0.5
Tints of Red		
▬	3354	0.5
◆	3687	1
⋌	3688	1
Tints of Yellow		
U	743	0.5
/	745	Small amount
◢	783	″
‖	972	″
Tints of Blue		
■	312	Small amount
◻	334	0.5
⊥	793	0.5
S	794	0.5
Brown △	3064	Small amount
Ash gray ◑	415	″

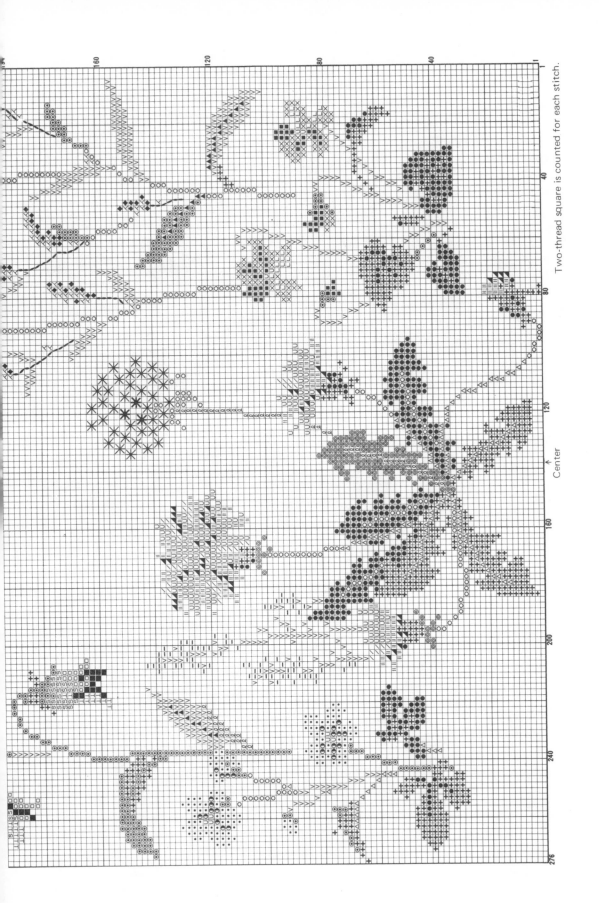

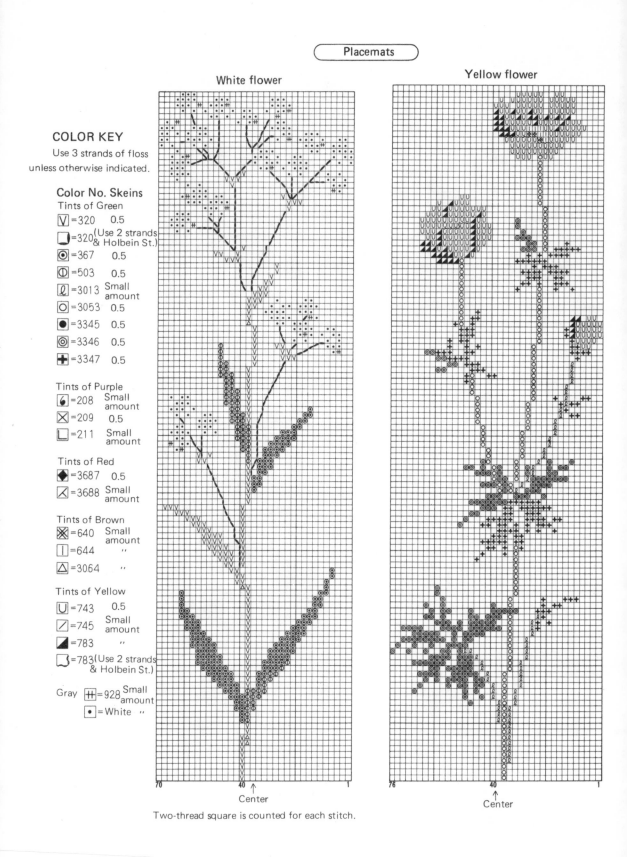

Placemats

White flower

Yellow flower

COLOR KEY

Use 3 strands of floss
unless otherwise indicated.

Color No. Skeins
Tints of Green
Ⅴ =320   0.5
☐ =320 (Use 2 strands
           & Holbein St.)
◉ =367   0.5
Ⓘ =503   0.5
ℓ =3013   Small amount
O =3053   0.5
● =3345   0.5
◎ =3346   0.5
✚ =3347   0.5

Tints of Purple
◖ =208   Small amount
✕ =209   0.5
⌴ =211   Small amount

Tints of Red
◆ =3687   0.5
⟋ =3688   Small amount

Tints of Brown
✖ =640   Small amount
∥ =644   ''
△ =3064   ''

Tints of Yellow
U =743   0.5
╱ =745   Small amount
◣ =783   ''
⏖ =783 (Use 2 strands
          & Holbein St.)

Gray ✛ =928 Small amount
     ⊡ =White ''

70   40   ↑   1
            Center

76   40   ↑   1
            Center

Two-thread square is counted for each stitch.

88

Purple flower

84   40   1
↑
Center

Pink flower

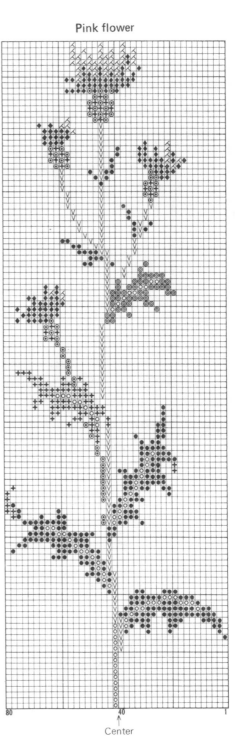

80   40   1
↑
Center

Doll House Panel, *shown on page 27.*

MATERIALS: Beige linen (130 vertical and horizontal threads per 10cm square), 43cm by 20.5cm. D.M.C. 6-strand embroidery floss, No. 25: See Color Key for colors and amounts. Cotton fabric and cardboard, 13.5cm by 36cm each. One pair of hanging tacks.

Two-thread square is counted for each stitch.

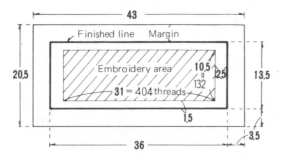

Cut cotton fabric same as finished size.

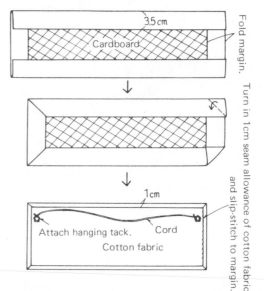

FINISHED SIZE: 13.5cm by 36cm.
DIRECTIONS: Find center point of each design
and work in cross-stitch, following chart. Make
up for panel, following directions on page 90.

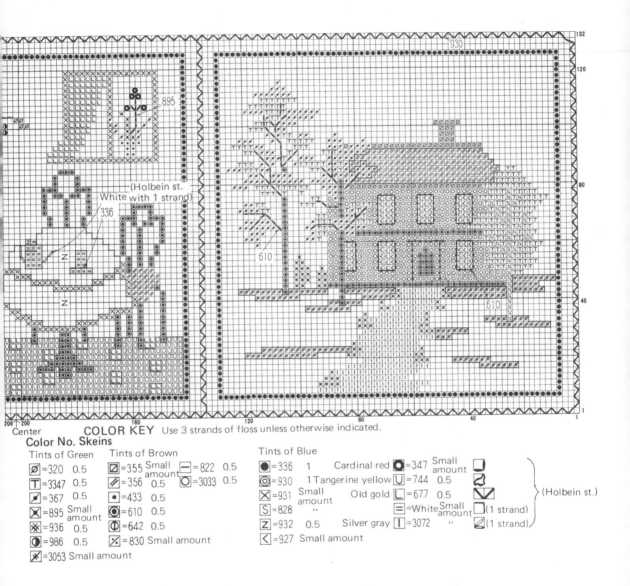

following directions on page 90.

Center

COLOR KEY Use 3 strands of floss unless otherwise indicated.

Color No. Skeins

Tints of Green		Tints of Brown			Tints of Blue				
⊘=320	0.5	☒=355 Small amount	▬=822	0.5	●=336	1	Cardinal red 🌑=347 Small amount		◻
T=3347	0.5	▨=356 0.5	⭗=3033	0.5	◎=930	1	Tangerine yellow U=744 0.5		⊋
▰=367	0.5	•=433	0.5		X=931 Small amount		Old gold L=677 0.5		▽ (Holbein st.)
X=895 Small amount		◉=610	0.5		S=828 "		⊟=White Small amount		◻(1 strand)
✻=936	0.5	Φ=642	0.5		Z=932	0.5	Silver gray ▯=3072 "		◪(1 strand)
◐=986	0.5	╱=830 Small amount			≪=927 Small amount				
✗=3053 Small amount									

Napkins, Doily and Coasters,

shown on pages 22 and 23.

MATERIALS: Sepia Indian cloth (52 vertical and horizontal threads per 10cm square), 86cm by 86cm square for 3 napkins, 3 coasters, and 1 doily. D.M.C. 6-strand embroidery floss, No. 25: See Color Key for colors and amounts.

FINISHED SIZE: Napkin, 43cm by 43cm square. Doily, 30cm by 30cm square. Coaster, 13cm by 13cm square.

DIRECTIONS: FOR NAPKIN, DOILY AND COASTER: Select embroidery area by counting threads of fabric. Work in cross-stitch, following chart. Draw 8 threads from fabric on all edges for fringe.

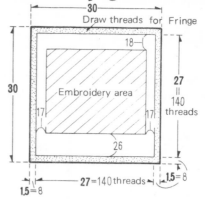

Doily

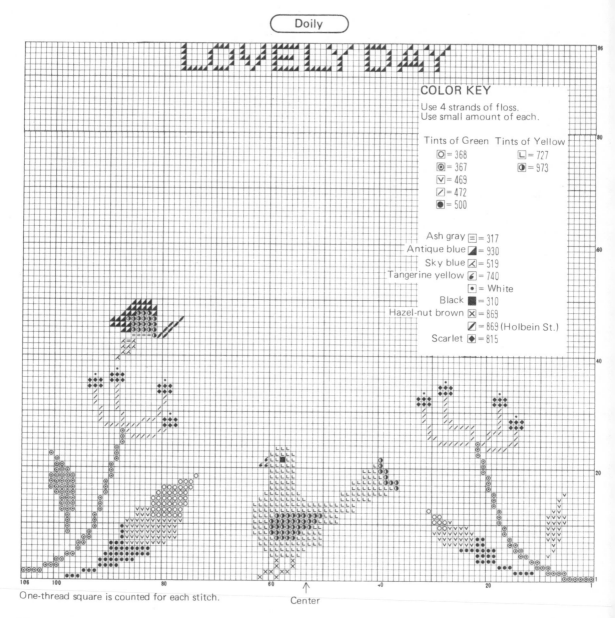

COLOR KEY

Use 4 strands of floss.
Use small amount of each.

Tints of Green | Tints of Yellow
- ◯ = 368
- ◉ = 367
- ∨ = 469
- ⧄ = 472
- ⬤ = 500
- ⌐ = 727
- ◑ = 973

Ash gray ⊟ = 317
Antique blue ◪ = 930
Sky blue ⊠ = 519
Tangerine yellow ▨ = 740
• = White
Black ■ = 310
Hazel-nut brown ⊠ = 869
⧄ = 869 (Holbein St.)
Scarlet ◆ = 815

One-thread square is counted for each stitch.

Center

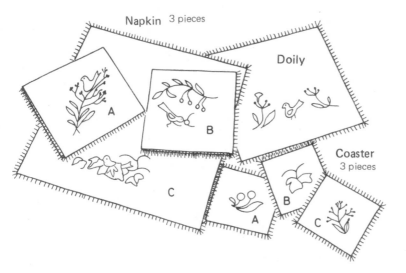

Napkin 3 pieces

Doily

Coaster 3 pieces

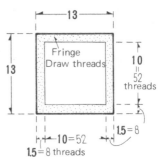

13

13

10 = 52 threads

Fringe
Draw threads

10 = 52
1.5 = 8 threads

1.5 = 8

Coaster

A

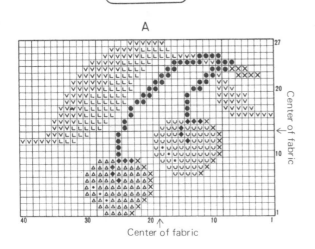

Center of fabric

Center of fabric

One-thread square is counted for each stitch.

COLOR KEY

Use 4 strands of floss.
Use small amount of each.

Tints of Green	Tints of Pink
O = 368	△ = 223
◉ = 367	U = 224
V = 469	◆ = 815
● = 500	S = 899

Hazelnut brown X = 869
Saffron L = 727
• = White

B

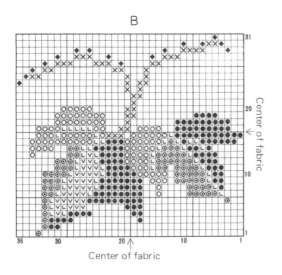

Center of fabric

Center of fabric

C

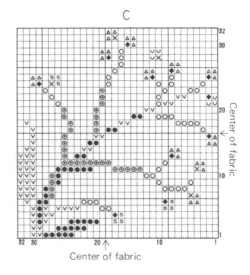

Center of fabric

Center of fabric

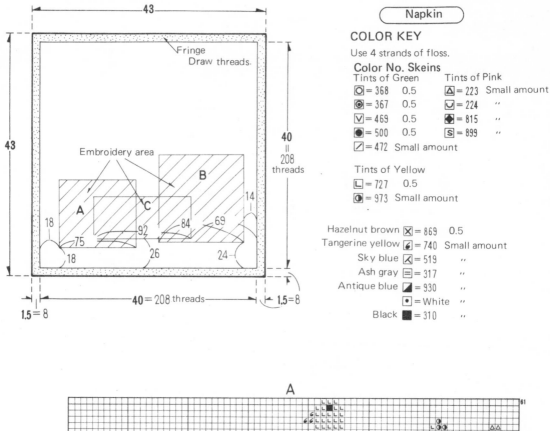

COLOR KEY

Use 4 strands of floss.

Color No. Skeins

Tints of Green		Tints of Pink	
○ = 368	0.5	△ = 223	Small amount
◉ = 367	0.5	∪ = 224	″
V = 469	0.5	◆ = 815	″
● = 500	0.5	S = 899	″
⊘ = 472	Small amount		

Tints of Yellow	
L = 727	0.5
◑ = 973	Small amount

Hazelnut brown	✕ = 869	0.5	
Tangerine yellow	◪ = 740	Small amount	
Sky blue	⊠ = 519	″	
Ash gray	☰ = 317	″	
Antique blue	◪ = 930	″	
	⊡ = White	″	
Black	■ = 310	″	

A

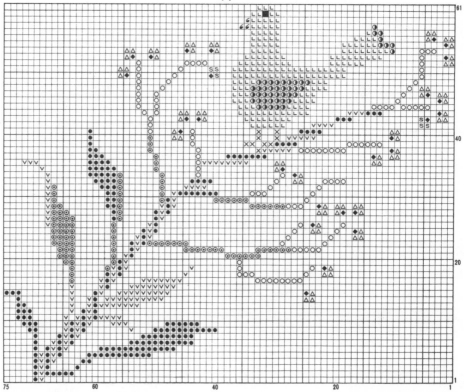

One-thread square is counted for each stitch.

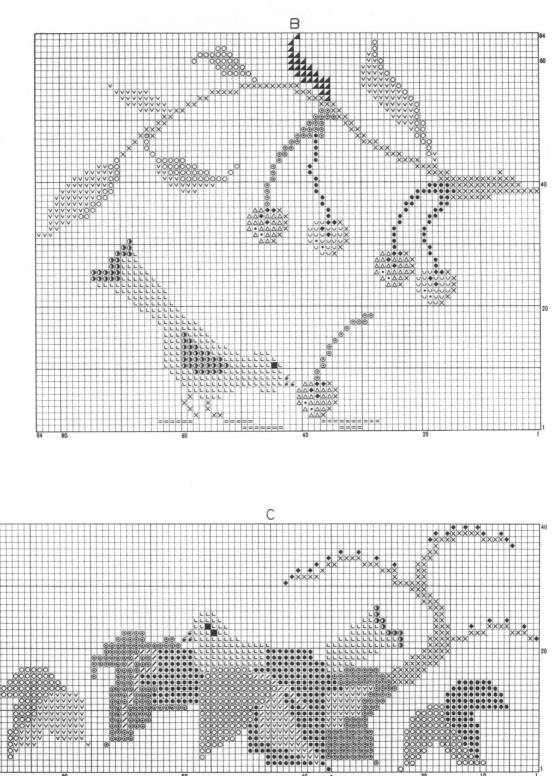

Center of fabric

Bridge Panel, *shown on page 29.*

MATERIALS: Blue Aida cloth (41 vertical and horizontal threads per 10cm square), 58cm by 42cm. D.M.C. 6-strand embroidery floss, No. 25: See Color Key for colors and amounts.
FINISHED SIZE: 27cm by 43cm (embroidery area).

DIRECTIONS: Find center point of fabric and work in cross-stitch, following chart. Mount and frame.

COLOR KEY

Use 3 strands of floss.

Color No. Skeins

Tints of Green

⊡ = 955	0.5
⊘ = 502	0.5
△ = 3347	0.5
◎ = 936	0.5

Tints of Red

▼ = 221	0.5
○ = 352	1
✳ = 3689	0.5

Indigo ● = 939	3.5
□ = 939 (Holbein St.)	
Light yellow ∨ = 3078 (1strand)	
Plum ✕ = 554	0.5
Antique blue ⊞ = 931	0.5
Beige N = 3022	0.5
⊡ = White	1

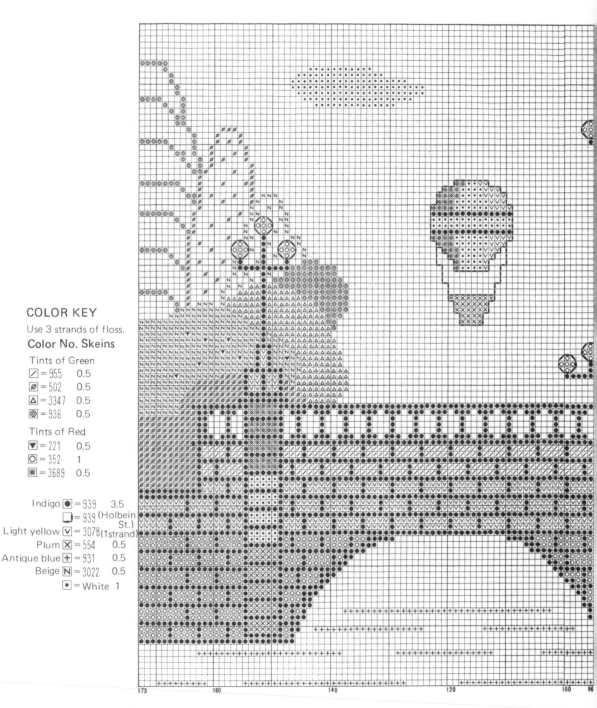

173   160   140   120   100 96

One-thread square is counted for each stitch.

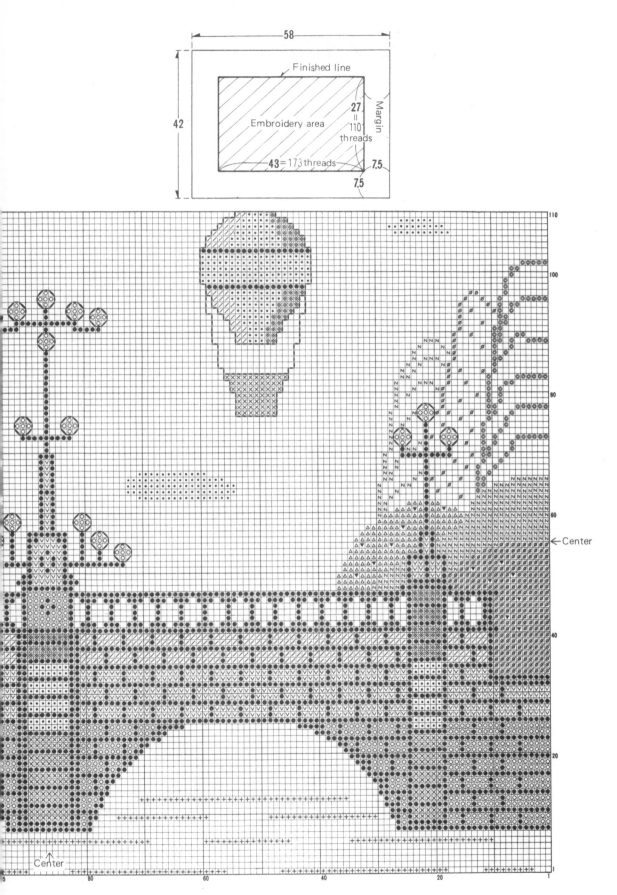

Petite Fleur Album, *shown on page 31.*

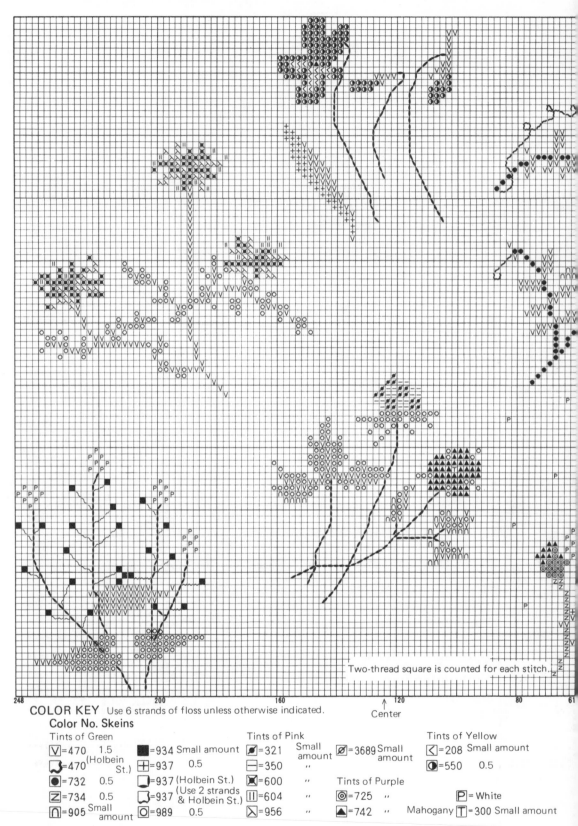

Two-thread square is counted for each stitch.

248 200 160 120 80 61

↑
Center

COLOR KEY Use 6 strands of floss unless otherwise indicated.
Color No. Skeins

Tints of Green

V =470	1.5
■ =934	Small amount
470 (Holbein St.)	
● =732	0.5
+ =937	0.5
□ =937 (Holbein St.)	
Z =734	0.5
937 (Use 2 strands & Holbein St.)	
∩ =905	Small amount
O =989	0.5

Tints of Pink

◢ =321	Small amount
⊟ =350	"
✕ =600	"
Ⅲ =604	"
✕ =956	"

| ⊘ =3689 | Small amount |

Tints of Purple

| ◎ =725 | " |
| ▲ =742 | " |

Tints of Yellow

| < =208 | Small amount |
| ◐ =550 | 0.5 |

P = White

Mahogany T =300 Small amount

98

MATERIALS: Natural-colored Oxford cloth (79 vertical and horizontal threads per 10cm square), 46cm by 95cm. D.M.C. 6-strand embroidery floss, No. 25: See Color Key for colors and amounts.

FINISHED SIZE: 36cm by 42cm.

DIRECTIONS: Determine embroidery area by counting threads of fabric. Work in cross-stitch, following chart. You may need a professional's help to finish the album.

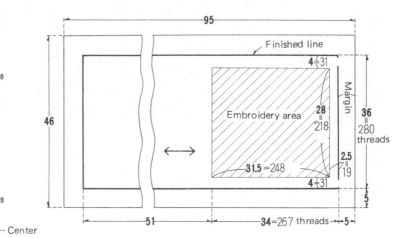

← Center

Flower Garden Album,

shown on page 30.

MATERIALS: Natural-colored Indian cloth (52 vertical and horizontal threads per 10cm square), 75.5cm by 44cm. D.M.C. 6-strand embroidery floss, No. 25: See Color Key for colors and amounts.

FINISHED SIZE: 31cm by 34cm.

DIRECTIONS: Select the embroidery area by counting threads of fabric. Work in cross-stitch, following chart. You may need a professional's help to finish the album.

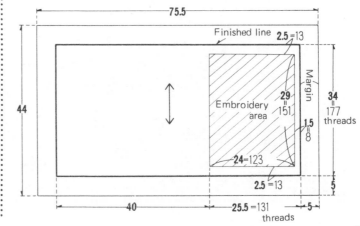

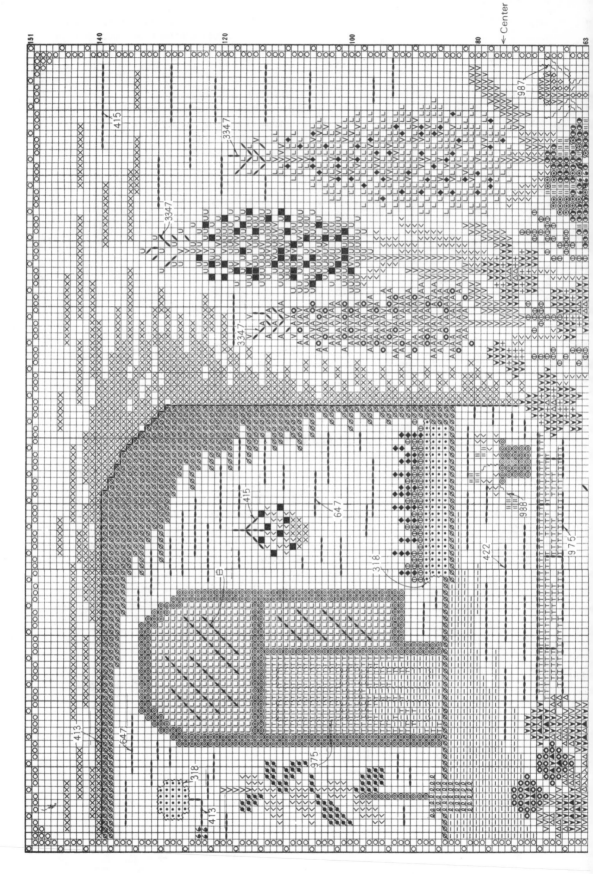

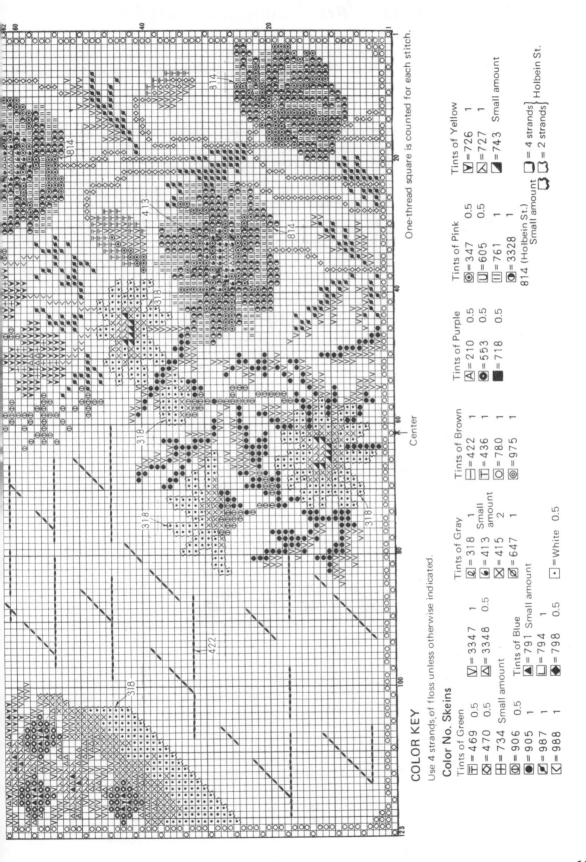

One-thread square is counted for each stitch.

COLOR KEY

Use 4 strands of floss unless otherwise indicated.

Color No. Skeins

Tints of Green

⊞ =469	0.5	▽ =3347	1
⊗ =470	0.5	△ =3348	0.5
⊞ =734	Small amount		
⊕ =906	0.5	**Tints of Blue**	
⊙ =905	1	▲ =791 Small amount	
◩ =987	1	⊔ =794	1
◿ =988	1	◆ =798	0.5

Tints of Gray

⊘ =318	1	
◕ =413	Small amount	
⊠ =415	2	
⊘ =647	1	

Tints of Brown

⊟ =422	1
⊤ =436	1
⊙ =780	1
⊚ =975	1

Tints of Purple

◮ =210	0.5
⊙ =553	0.5
■ =718	0.5

Tints of Pink

⊙ =347	0.5
⊔ =605	0.5
⫿ =761	1
⊘ =3328	1
814 (Holbein St.) Small amount	

Tints of Yellow

▼ =726	1
⊠ =727	1
◤ =743	Small amount

□ = 4 strands } Holbein St.
⊂⊃ = 2 strands }

□ =White 0.5

Rabbit Panel, *shown on page 27.*

MATERIALS: Navy Aida cloth (41 vertical and horizontal threads per 10cm square), 20cm by 18cm. D.M.C. 6-strand embroidery floss, No. 25: See Color Key for colors and amounts.

FINISHED SIZE: 20cm by 18cm.
DIRECTIONS: Find center point of fabric and work in cross-stitch, following chart. Mount and frame.

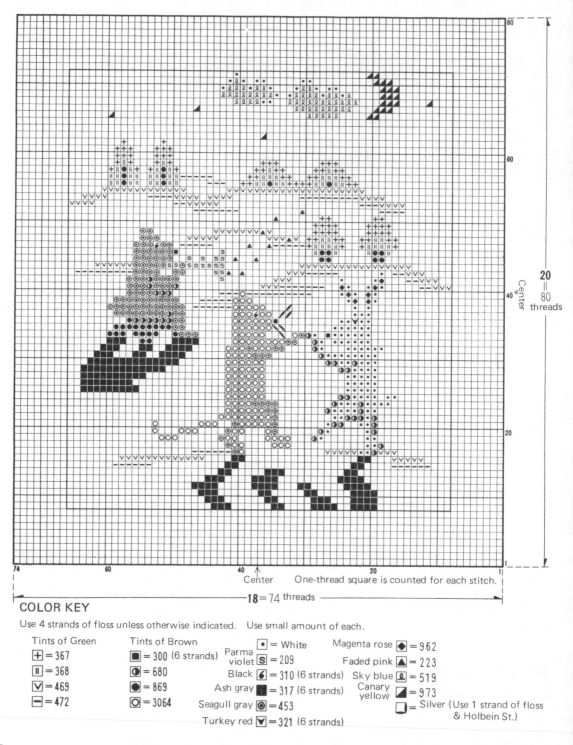

One-thread square is counted for each stitch.

18 = 74 threads

COLOR KEY

Use 4 strands of floss unless otherwise indicated.   Use small amount of each.

Tints of Green	Tints of Brown		
⊞ = 367	■ = 300 (6 strands)	Parma violet S = 209	Magenta rose ◆ = 962
‖ = 368	◑ = 680	Black ◪ = 310 (6 strands)	Faded pink ▲ = 223
☑ = 469	● = 869	Ash gray ▥ = 317 (6 strands)	Sky blue ⍩ = 519
⊟ = 472	○ = 3064	Seagull gray ◉ = 453	Canary yellow ◪ = 973
		Turkey red ▼ = 321 (6 strands)	□ = Silver (Use 1 strand of floss & Holbein St.)

Brown Slippers, *shown on page 32.*

MATERIALS: Sepia Congress canvas (70 vertical and horizontal threads per 10cm square), 54cm by 30cm. Brown linen (130 vertical and horizontal threads per 10cm square), 35cm by 30cm (for sole). D.M.C. 6-strand embroidery floss, No. 25: See Color Key for colors and amounts.

FINISHED SIZE: Foot size, 26cm.

DIRECTIONS: Select embroidery areas as shown and work in cross-stitch, following chart. Don't cut embroidered fabric. You may need professional help for finished slippers.

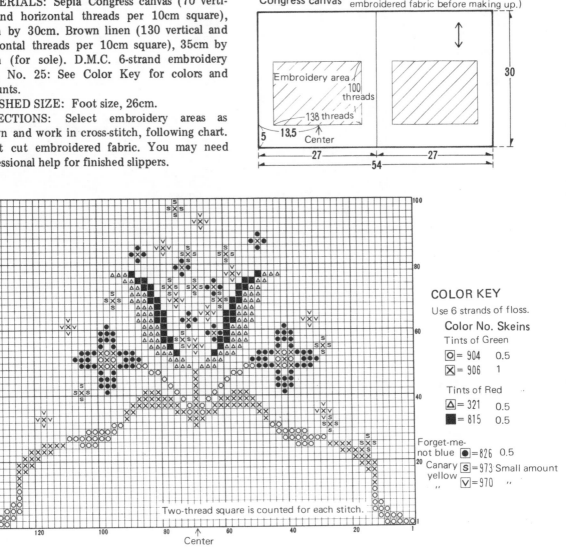

COLOR KEY

Use 6 strands of floss.

Color No. Skeins

Tints of Green

O = 904   0.5

X = 906   1

Tints of Red

△ = 321   0.5

■ = 815   0.5

Forget-me-not blue ● = 826 0.5

Canary yellow S = 973 Small amount

V = 970   „

Two-thread square is counted for each stitch.

Pink Slippers, *shown on page 32.*

MATERIALS: Rose pink Indian cloth (52 vertical and horizontal threads per 10cm square), 90cm by 30cm. D.M.C. 6-strand embroidery floss, No. 25: See Color Key for colors and amounts.

FINISHED SIZE: Foot size, 26cm.

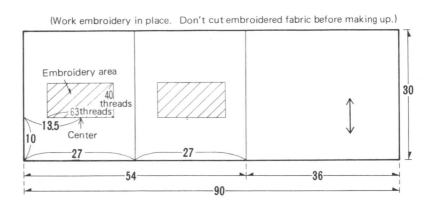

103

DIRECTIONS: Select embroidery area by counting threads of fabric and work in cross-stitch, following the chart. Don't cut fabric. You may need professional help for finished slippers.

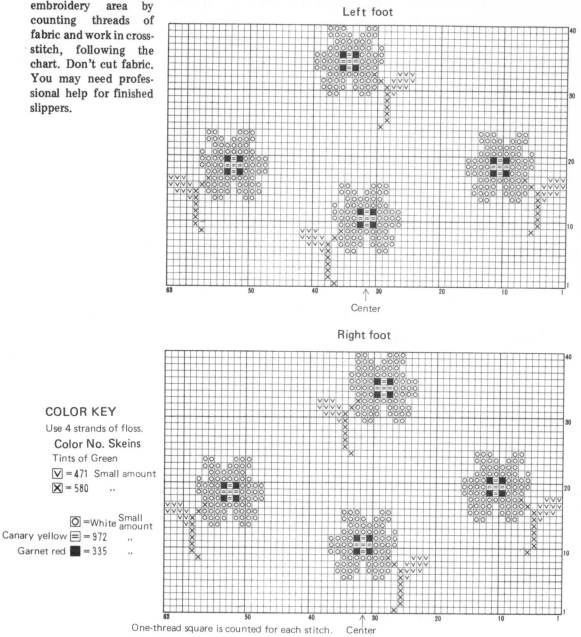

Left foot

Center

Right foot

COLOR KEY

Use 4 strands of floss.

Color No. Skeins

Tints of Green

$\boxed{V}$ = 471 Small amount

$\boxed{X}$ = 580   „

$\boxed{O}$ = White Small amount

Canary yellow $\boxed{=}$ = 972   „

Garnet red $\boxed{\blacksquare}$ = 335   „

One-thread square is counted for each stitch.   Center

BASICS IN CROSS STITCH

FABRICS

The exact amount of the fabric to make each project is given in this book. Make sure to buy enough fabric, allowing for shrinkage or difference of thread count.

Fineness or coarseness of the fabric will determine the finished size of the design.

To make the project the size shown in the book, use fabric with same gauge (the number of vertical and horizontal threads per 10cm square is given in the book). If you use coarser fabric than indicated, the finished size will be bigger and you may need more fabric. There are several kinds of fabric suitable for cross-stitch embroidery.

Cotton and linen fabrics on which you can count the threads easily are used most. Woolen and polyester fabrics are also used. Choose the most suitable even-weave fabric for your project.

Indian cloth and Java canvas are woven with several threads to each warp and weft. They are the most suitable fabrics for cross-stitch embroidery.

Congress canvas in woven with a single thick thread, thus this is a heavy-weight canvas. It is often used for cross-stitch embroidery and free-style embroidery with large stitches. Light-weight congress canvas is used for table-cloths with complicated embroidery.

Oxford cloth is often used for counted thread embroidery. This is an even-weave fabric and has double threads.

Even-weave linen comes in various thickness from fine to coarse. Light-weight linen is used for table linens with fine embroidery.

Length of Thread:

Use thread of 50cm length at a time, since longer thread may be tangled or twisted, which causes poor results and also causes the thread to lose its shine.

Starting Point:

Count the threads of the fabric and mark the starting point or center of design with colored thread. Make sure to count the threads of the fabric when embroidering repeating or symmetrical patterns.

THREADS

There are various kinds of threads used, depending on the thickness of the fabric.

Six-strand embroidery floss, No. 25, is most commonly used. Woolen yarn (tapestry yarn), and gold and silver threads are also used according to the texture of the fabric.

Six-strand embroidery floss, No. 25: This can be separated into one or more strands. When 3 strands of floss are required; for example, pull out one strand at a time and put three strands together. The length of one skein is 8 meters long.

Pearl cotton, No. 5: This is a shiny corded thread. The length of one skein is 25 meters long.

NEEDLES

You may use any needle for embroidery, but a blunt-pointed needle for cross-stitch embroidery is easiest to use. Change the size of the needle and the number of strands, depending on the fabric to be used.

To embroider with one strand of floss, use No. 23 needle for cross-stitch embroidery, and Nos. 19 and 20 needles for 4 to 6 strands of floss. Choose the proper needle and the number of strands suitable for the fabric and design.

Preparations:

The fabric suitable for cross-stitch embroidery frays easily, so overcast the edges with large stitches to prevent raveling.

How to Thread:

Fold the thread over the end of the needle, slip it off with thumb and forefinger and push it through the needle eye.

Fold the thread end.   Slip it off with thumb and forefinger.

To prevent the thread from twisting:

The thread is apt to twist while embroidering. To prevent this, turn the needle occasionally. Before starting, put the required number of strands together by pulling out one strand at a time from skein.

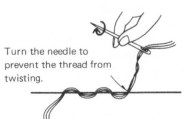

Turn the needle to prevent the thread from twisting.

Starting and Ending:

Leave the thread twice as long as the length of the needle on the wrong side when starting. After embroidering, weave the thread end into 2- to 3cm-stitches on the wrong side and clip off the excess thread. When you use various kinds of colored threads, weave and clip off any excess thread every time new thread is used.

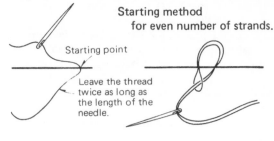

Starting method for even number of strands.

Starting point

Leave the thread twice as long as the length of the needle.

CROSS-STITCH

Make sure to work all the top threads of crosses in the same direction.
Never mix them up.

To work horizontally:

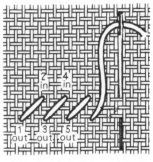

Bring the thread through on the lower left line of the cross. Insert the needle on the upper line a little to the right.

When coming to the end of the row, bring the thread through on the lower right line of the cross and insert the needle on the upper line a little to the left. Return in this way completing the other half of the cross.

Finish the first row, then proceed to the next row.

To complete each cross horizontally:

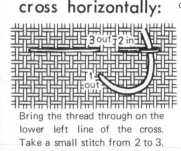

Bring the thread through on the lower left line of the cross. Take a small stitch from 2 to 3.

Insert the needle on the lower line a little to the right (at 4) emerging at 5.

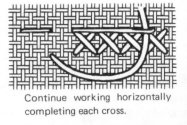

Continue working horizontally completing each cross.

To complete each cross vertically:

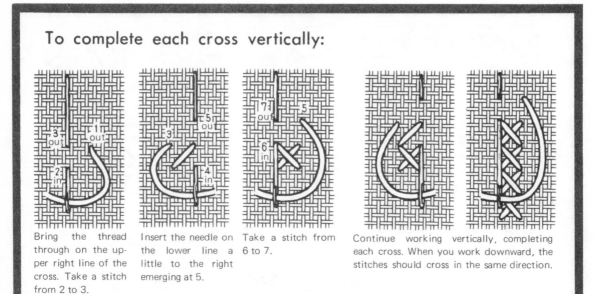

Bring the thread through on the upper right line of the cross. Take a stitch from 2 to 3.

Insert the needle on the lower line a little to the right emerging at 5.

Take a stitch from 6 to 7.

Continue working vertically, completing each cross. When you work downward, the stitches should cross in the same direction.

To work upward diagonally:

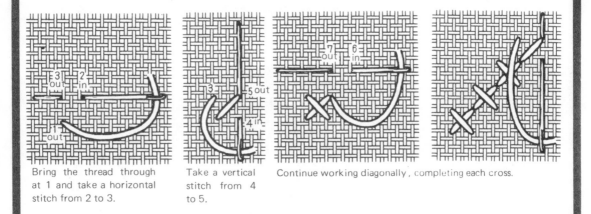

Bring the thread through at 1 and take a horizontal stitch from 2 to 3.

Take a vertical stitch from 4 to 5.

Continue working diagonally, completing each cross.

To work downward diagonally:

 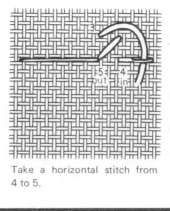 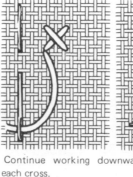 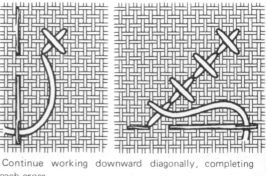

Bring the thread through at 1 and take a vertical stitch from 2 to 3.

Take a horizontal stitch from 4 to 5.

Continue working downward diagonally, completing each cross.

DOUBLE CROSS-STITCH

Work Cross-Stitch first. Then work another Cross-Stitch over the previous stitch as shown. All stitches should cross in the same way.

HOLBEIN STITCH

This is also called Line Stitch and is sometimes used as an outline to Cross-Stitch. The stitch is completed by working from left to right and coming back from right to left. Stitches on the wrong side are the same on the front.

Straight Line:

Work running stitch of equal length.

When you come to the end of the row, return in the same way filling in the spaces left by the first row. For a neater finish, work in the same way when you insert the needle and bring it through.

Diagonal Line:

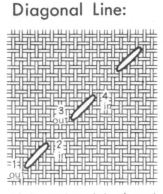

Work running stitch of equal length diagonally.

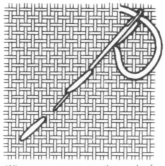

When you come to the end of the row, return in the same way filling in the spaces left by the first row.

Zigzag Line:

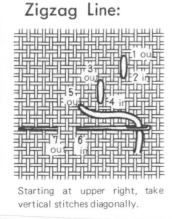

Starting at upper right, take vertical stitches diagonally.

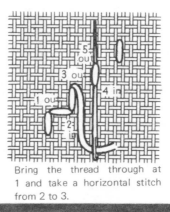

Bring the thread through at 1 and take a horizontal stitch from 2 to 3.

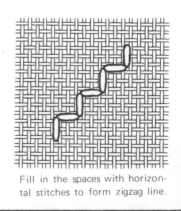

Fill in the spaces with horizontal stitches to form zigzag line.

HOW TO MAKE HEM

Hem-stitch

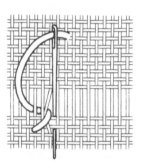

1. Draw out required number of threads from the fabric in both directions.
2. Miter corners and slip-stitch. Baste four sides.
3. Hem-stitch along drawn thread line. (Buttonhole-stitch at corners.)

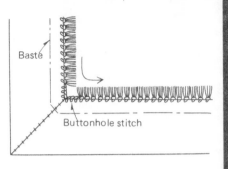

Baste

Buttonhole stitch

Bring the needle out close to the drawn thread line and pick up threads from right to left. Bring the needle in vertically and pull the thread in needle taut. Repeat these steps.

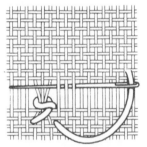

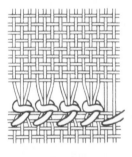

MITERED CORNER

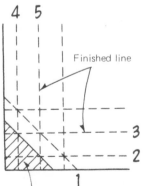

4 5

Finished line

3
2
1

Cut off the corner as indicated.
Fold in numerical order.

4 5

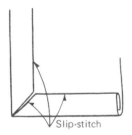

Slip-stitch